Worthing Swimming Club

(Affiliated to the S.L.C.A.S.A., the S.C.W.P.A., and the Life Saving Society).

PROGRAMME OF ENTERTAINMENT

For the Benefit of

Mr. MARTIN STREETER, the Bath Attendant,

At 7 o'clock sharp,

On WEDNESDAY, Oct. 24th, 1900,

At THE BATHS, WEST WORTHING.

Judges : F. PARISH, Esq. (President W.S.C.), Councillor G. EWEN SMITH, Mr. A. F. WALTER, Mr. J. BLAKER.

Starter : Mr. T. J. LYNE. Timekeeper : Mr. T. H. GREET.

Referee : Mr. R. C. PAINE. Handicapper : Mr. E. J. DEAN.

FIGHT FOR THE SUSSEX SENIOR CHAMPIONSHIP.

The Final Match for this Competition will take place at **HOVE**, on Wednesday Evening Next, Oct. 31st. Cheap Train at 6.40.

This painting by E. Martin of Tarring in 1856 is one of the earliest pictures of a game of stoolball in progress. The 'stool' being used as a wicket looks very like a milking stool, and in a relaxed atmosphere men and women are playing mixed teams.

WORTHING PAST

Sally White

Phillimore

2000

Published by
PHILLIMORE & CO. LTD.
Shopwyke Manor Barn, Chichester, West Sussex

ISBN 1 86077 146 7

Printed and bound in Great Britain by
BIDDLES LTD.
Guildford, Surrey

This book is dedicated with affection and gratitude to three men called John.
Without them it could never have been written.
It is in memory of John Norwood who nurtured my career,
for John Bergin who fought for it
and above all for John Manley who has transformed my life.

Contents

List of Illustrations

Frontispiece: Tarring in 1856

Acknowledgements

I am very grateful to the following for granting me permission to reproduce illustrations: Beryl Heryet 5, 6; Joan Pinker 166; The Sussex Archaeological Society 3, 4; Beckett Newspapers 7, 150, 161, 162; The *Brighton Evening Argus* 43, 154; Francis Frith Collection 81, 100, 127, 128, 158, 168; Walter Gardiner Photography 9, 15, 65, 69, 73, 74, 79, 89, 97, 101, 109, 112, 120, 121, 129, 133, 143, 146, 147, 151, 152, 153, 167; and Worthing Museum and Art Gallery for all the other illustrations apart from 1, 23, 68, 72, 116, 169 which are my own.

In learning about Worthing I have benefited from years of fruitful collaboration and contact with staff at Worthing Library, the *Worthing Herald*, *Brighton Evening Argus* and the *West Sussex Gazette*, as well as countless members of the public who have shared nuggets of information with me.

I owe a huge debt of thanks to many people who have supported me during the writing of this book: Elda Elliot, John Roles, Charles Miles-Read, Val and Jim Peters, Jim Shields, Derek and Doreen Painter, Ian Montgomery, friends and colleagues in various museums, Jane Doré from Worthing Library; and above all to my Mum, to my sister Lisa and to Barney.

Introduction

I am an incomer but, that being said, I have known Worthing since 1956 when my mother struggled to occupy my elder brother and myself while my father had a summer job as a seafront photographer with Happy Snaps at 1 Marine Parade. Throughout my childhood most of our holidays were spent in nearby Storrington and a visit to Peter Pan's Playground on Worthing seafront was an eagerly awaited treat. After a long gap chance brought me back. I wanted a job in a museum and John Norwood gave me the break I was looking for and employed me. In the 16 years I have worked here my childhood affection for the town and its surrounding countryside has deepened into a real love.

Worthing, I often say, is a town that grows on you. I have lost count of the people I have met who moved here to work, meaning to stay only a short while and then move on. Years later they are still here, choosing to stay. Worthing remains what it has long been, a nice place to live. Some people bemoan the influx of outsiders in the 20th century. I, on the other hand, am delighted to see how the mix of people of all ages and from a widening range of backgrounds has enriched the population of Worthing and shaped it better for moving into the new millennium.

It is worth remembering that Worthing is a relatively young town. Little more than two hundred years ago it consisted of a cluster of huts and shacks. This means that even the families with the oldest connection to Worthing can only trace their families back a bit more than two centuries. I sometimes think that this has contributed to what I, as an incomer, see as a kind of inbuilt inferiority complex in local residents. It is as if they regard the fact that the town lacks many centuries of continuous history as a weakness, something they have to apologise for when comparing Worthing with its neighbours. Worthing has a great deal

more history than immediately meets the eye. In tracing the development of this patch of land since the Stone Age, I will show not only that occupation of the area has been more or less continuous, but also that it can justifiably claim to have the oldest known industrial-scale production site in the country.

The modern Borough of Worthing stretches along the coast from Goring in the west to Brooklands in the east. To the north it includes Durrington, High Salvington, Findon Valley and Broadwater. For the purposes of this book two sites, Highdown Hill and Cissbury will be included which sit outside, but adjacent to, the Borough boundary. It is not my purpose here to record every detail of land ownership, taxation, political allegiance or building in the development of Worthing, nor to list every influential person who has contributed to its growth but, rather, to try to give a flavour of each phase in its development, highlighting events or personalities of particular interest and illustrating them with a mixture of well-known and lesser known pictures. I hope that reading the book and looking at the pictures will give readers further reason to appreciate Worthing's story and to enjoy its present.

1 The author on her first visit to Worthing in 1956, riding one of Mrs. Booth's ponies on the beach.

Prehistoric to Roman Worthing

South-east England lay under the sea about 100 million years ago. A thick layer of white calcareous mud was gradually laid down on the seabed. In time it was consolidated into chalk. Within the chalk, particles of silica, which had also been deposited, dissolved and were redeposited as layers of flint. During the Alpine upheaval that affected vast areas of Europe, parts of this area were uplifted, forming rounded hills. Water eroded much of the chalk away, leaving the Downs as a rim of hills around the lower area of the Weald. Along the coastal plain water exposed clays and sands which were then covered by gravel topped by a very fertile wind-blown deposit called brickearth. The centre of modern Worthing lies on the coastal plain with High Salvington and Durrington on the gentle southern slopes of the South Downs.

It is clear from isolated finds which continue to be made throughout the Borough that the Worthing area has been occupied for a very long time. However, the finds are patchy from all periods which pre-date the keeping of detailed written records and we get very little insight into the transition between phases and periods or into the details of the daily life of the people who lived here. A few flint tools from the Old Stone Age have been found in Goring, High Salvington

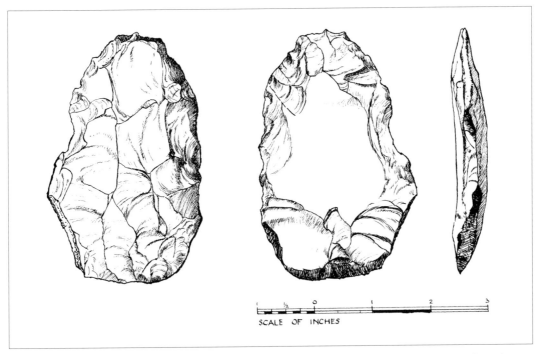

SCALE OF INCHES

2 Flint tools dating from the Old Stone Age are not common in Worthing. This axe, shown from three different angles, was found in Broadwater.

1

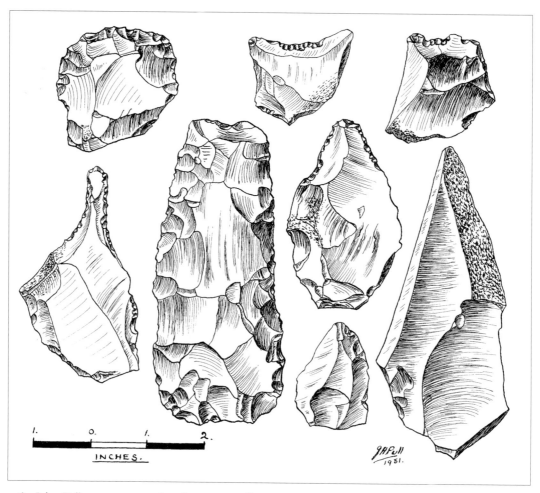

6 John Pull was an expert draughtsman as well as excavator and drew these flint tools which he had excavated. A small group of other archaeologists said that his drawings were not good enough to be published in the local archaeological journal. The high standards that he set are now being recognised by modern archaeologists.

woodland being cleared for the establishment of farms, that stock keeping and cultivation led to the building of permanent settlements, and that spinning, weaving and pottery-making were introduced. We also know that, at least sometimes, the people built mounds of earth over their dead. No traces of these aspects of life have been found around Worthing, apart from a few pieces of broken pottery and some animal bones. What we do have are huge numbers of flint tools at all stages of manufacture and those which have been used and broken. These people had an impressive range of specialised tools including axes, fine arrowheads, sickles, knives, scrapers and saws. We know that there was some trade between local

people and those in other parts of the country since axes made of Sussex flint have been found in distant parts of England and others, made of types of stone such as dolerite which does not occur naturally in Sussex, have been found here. What these changes in lifestyle do illustrate is that the people who lived here were capable of organising themselves to co-operate on large-scale projects which would benefit the whole community.

Some years before 2000 B.C., people who had learnt how to work bronze arrived in this country and their techniques were gradually adopted throughout the country. They also brought more advanced methods of pottery

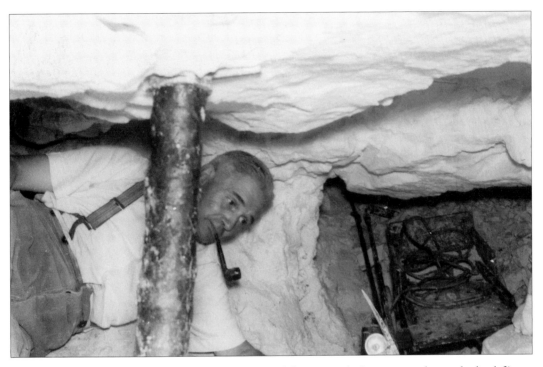

5 John Pull was a gifted amateur archaeologist who did more work than anyone else on the local flint mines. This picture shows him working in cramped conditions in one of the side galleries at Cissbury in the 1950s.

into a subsistence economy based on farming. No settlements from this period have yet been found around Worthing. However, it can claim to be the site of the oldest known industrial-scale production centre in England.

Cissbury Ring, better known to many people for its Iron-Age hillfort, was the site of well over a hundred flint mine shafts which have been radio-carbon dated to *c*.4000-3000 B.C. Flint occurs in either even tabular bands or layers of nodules throughout the chalk. In earlier periods people had used flints found on the surface for their tools but this flint has been weathered and it was real-ised that mined flint was better for making at least some tools. The mines were dug using antlers as pickaxes, wedges and hammers, and shoulder blades as shovels. The mines were up to 13 metres deep and some of them have galleries radiating out from the base of the shaft. Although traces of soot from lamps which burnt fat have been found on the ceilings of a few galleries, it is thought that most of the work was done by daylight reflecting off the white chalk. It is not clear how the chalk and flint were carried to the surface.

The mines at Cissbury were first recognised by Colonel Lane Fox (better known as General Pitt Rivers) in 1867 and 1875. He found that some of the shafts underlay the ramparts of the hillfort and therefore pre-dated it. He also dug deeply enough through the rubble which had filled the shaft to recognise it as a mine. A number of further excavations have taken place in the mines, the most recent being by gifted amateur archaeologist John Pull in the 1950s. There are still big gaps in our knowledge of how the mines were worked. We do not know if the mining was seasonal; or if, like tasks such as pottery making and weaving, it was done by specialists or whether it involved the whole community; we do not even know if the miners were men, women or both. John Pull found the skeleton of a young woman in a side gallery at the bottom of one of the Cissbury shafts. She appeared to have been killed by a rock fall from the roof of the gallery.

We know frustratingly little about the people who worked the mines. We know from other areas that the New Stone Age saw large areas of

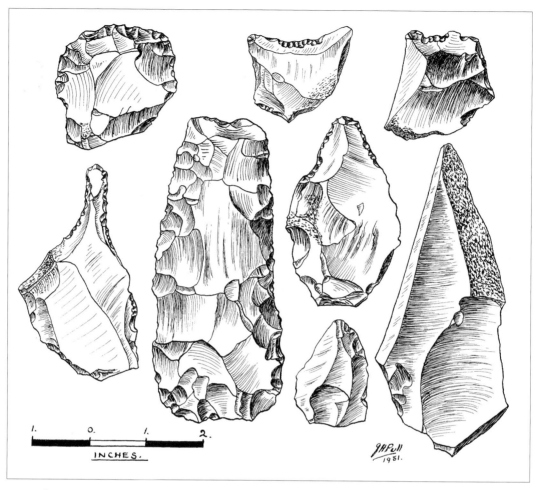

6 John Pull was an expert draughtsman as well as excavator and drew these flint tools which he had excavated. A small group of other archaeologists said that his drawings were not good enough to be published in the local archaeological journal. The high standards that he set are now being recognised by modern archaeologists.

woodland being cleared for the establishment of farms, that stock keeping and cultivation led to the building of permanent settlements, and that spinning, weaving and pottery-making were introduced. We also know that, at least sometimes, the people built mounds of earth over their dead. No traces of these aspects of life have been found around Worthing, apart from a few pieces of broken pottery and some animal bones. What we do have are huge numbers of flint tools at all stages of manufacture and those which have been used and broken. These people had an impressive range of specialised tools including axes, fine arrowheads, sickles, knives, scrapers and saws. We know that there was some trade between local

people and those in other parts of the country since axes made of Sussex flint have been found in distant parts of England and others, made of types of stone such as dolerite which does not occur naturally in Sussex, have been found here. What these changes in lifestyle do illustrate is that the people who lived here were capable of organising themselves to co-operate on large-scale projects which would benefit the whole community.

Some years before 2000 B.C., people who had learnt how to work bronze arrived in this country and their techniques were gradually adopted throughout the country. They also brought more advanced methods of pottery

One

Prehistoric to Roman Worthing

South-east England lay under the sea about 100 million years ago. A thick layer of white calcareous mud was gradually laid down on the seabed. In time it was consolidated into chalk. Within the chalk, particles of silica, which had also been deposited, dissolved and were redeposited as layers of flint. During the Alpine upheaval that affected vast areas of Europe, parts of this area were uplifted, forming rounded hills. Water eroded much of the chalk away, leaving the Downs as a rim of hills around the lower area of the Weald. Along the coastal plain water exposed clays and sands which were then covered by gravel topped by a very fertile wind-blown deposit called brickearth. The centre of modern Worthing lies on the coastal plain with High Salvington and Durrington on the gentle southern slopes of the South Downs.

It is clear from isolated finds which continue to be made throughout the Borough that the Worthing area has been occupied for a very long time. However, the finds are patchy from all periods which pre-date the keeping of detailed written records and we get very little insight into the transition between phases and periods or into the details of the daily life of the people who lived here. A few flint tools from the Old Stone Age have been found in Goring, High Salvington

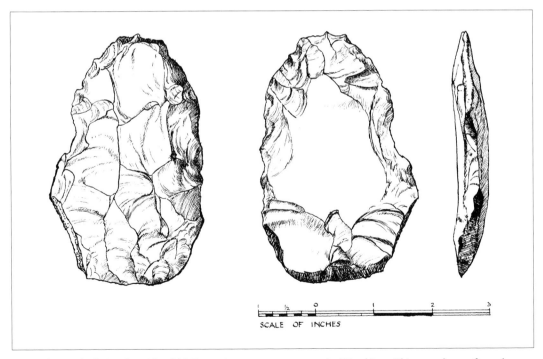

2 Flint tools dating from the Old Stone Age are not common in Worthing. This axe, shown from three different angles, was found in Broadwater.

1

3 This must be an early example of experimental archaeology. A group of schoolgirls and archaeologists at Harrow Hill in the 1920s appear to be finding how many schoolgirls it takes to lift a basket of chalk and flint to the surface. Health and Safety were obviously not the archaeologists' main concerns.

and Broadwater but there is no real sign that the area was settled in either the Old or Middle Stone Ages. However, since the people at that time were hunters and gatherers, moving around throughout the year to wherever food was available, and living in temporary camps, it is probable that groups visited the area from time to time, without leaving visible traces of their visits. It is likely that people were in this area at the time that Boxgrove near Chichester was occupied over 400,000 years ago. Because these people built no permanent settlements they left even fewer traces than their successors for archaeologists to uncover.

Around 8000 B.C. there was a sustained period of warming which caused large parts of the ice sheets in northern Europe to melt, producing a dramatic rise in the sea level of up to 10 metres in some parts of Britain. It was in this period that Britain was finally separated from the Continent. The warmer weather enabled a wider variety of plants and animals to live here and by 6000 B.C. most of south-east England was forested with oak, elm, alder, lime, hazel, ash and holly.

The New Stone Age began in c.4400 B.C. and was a period of enormous cultural change. It was also the first period from which we have real traces of occupation in the Worthing area. Adopting ideas which had spread from the European mainland, the local inhabitants made their first attempts to modify the environment which had hitherto controlled much of their lives. In time they transformed their hunter-gatherer lifestyle

4 In 1875 General Pitt Rivers excavated a section through the ramparts of the Iron-Age hillfort at Cissbury and revealed the top of a New Stone Age flint mine underneath the fortifications. This was the first time anyone had shown that the mines were older than the ramparts.

7 This hoard of 12 bronze palstaves and two socketed axes was found in a gravel pit in South Farm Road in 1928. One of the socketed axes fits almost perfectly into a mould which was found in Castle Road. The hoard can be dated to *c*.1500-1000 B.C.

making. Although this period is known as the Bronze Age, it naturally took time for this new technology to be adopted throughout the country and flint continued to be used for some time. Like anything new, bronze would have been particularly valuable at first and used for luxury items and a few craftsmen's tools rather than everyday objects. Bronze is an alloy of copper and tin, neither of which can be found in this area. Any bronze items found here therefore imply that some people, possibly the bronze workers themselves, travelled considerable distances to trade.

Farming communities continued to develop and in this area farms have been found at New Barn Down and Blackpatch, north of Worthing. People lived in round or oval houses made of a combination of upright posts and wattle and daub,

presumably with a thatched roof. Some settlements were surrounded with banks and palisades that could have been designed to keep out wild animals which could damage crops and stock as well as for protection against other people. The first enclosure on Highdown is thought to date to the late Bronze Age, around 1400-1200 B.C. It encloses 1 hectare, which makes it the largest late Bronze-Age enclosure in Sussex. It is roughly rectangular in shape and was enclosed by a bank and ditch. The ditch was originally about 4 metres wide, 2 metres deep and had a flat bottom. In the north-west area of the enclosure a round hut dated to the very end of the Bronze Age, *c*.900-600 B.C. was found. The function of the enclosure is unclear but it may have been a centre for the redistribution of goods. A late Bronze-Age hoard which may have belonged to a carpenter was found on Highdown in 1901 and 1902. It contained two small bronze chisels, a gouge, one dagger and parts of two others, and a gold hair ornament. In 1939 excavations through the rampart revealed the remains of two late Bronze-Age huts.

Within Worthing itself, the only traces of settlement which have been found so far are a few ditches containing pieces of late Bronze-Age pottery in the area around High Street and others in Durrington. That there were people in the area is shown by the discovery of an urn containing the cremated bones of a woman at Charmandean in Broadwater, another in Broadwater cemetery and by a number of hoards. Hoards were buried for a number of purposes, many of which we still fail to recognise. Some, often called Founder's Hoards, are thought to have belonged to itinerant bronze workers who could not carry their stock of raw materials with them at all times and buried them for safe-keeping while carrying samples to show the various communities and take orders for new tools and weapons. One such hoard may be the one which was found in the Forty Acres Brickfield near Ham Road. It was found by E.C. Patching in 1877. There were 28 palstaves, 10 socketed axes, one winged axe and two cakes of bronze in a pot. Sadly, the pot and some of the bronze items were dispersed but the majority, including the cakes of bronze, ended up in Worthing Museum and Art Gallery (Worthing Museum). Actual bronze-working in the area is illustrated by the discovery of a small crucible in South Farm Road and a two-piece mould for a socketed axe in Castle Road. The mould is an almost perfect fit for a socketed axe from the hoard which was found about two kilometres away from Castle Road in a gravel pit in South Farm Road in 1928. This hoard contained both palstaves and socketed axes and only one of them showed any signs of wear, the others looking as if they had come straight from their moulds.

The Iron Age, the period in which iron began to be used in England, began in c.700 B.C. and once again the new technology was introduced from the Continent. Unlike bronze, iron is not an alloy of different metals and might, therefore, be assumed to be easier to work. However, iron has a very high melting point and the temperatures needed for smelting it could not be reached until the use of charcoal had been discovered. Iron can

be hammered into shape and can be re-sharpened which gives it real advantages over bronze for making tools and weapons.

By the middle of the Iron Age the climate was similar to today and many of the plants which are familiar to us were common then. People lived in roundhouses and were efficient farmers, developing a plough called an 'ard' which could be pulled by oxen. Traces of Iron-Age fields can be seen on many parts of the South Downs. During the first century B.C. the potter's wheel was introduced. This meant that pottery would be produced in larger quantities and more standardised forms than before. It also extended the range of vessel types which could be made. Traces of Iron-Age occupation in Worthing are almost non-existent, limited to a couple of coins and beads and a quern (for grinding corn), although two important sites sit on its outskirts.

The late Bronze-Age enclosure on Highdown was reinforced in the early Iron Age, around 600 B.C., when a second rampart and ditch were added around the south and east. There are two entrances through the ramparts, to the east and south-west. Iron-Age enclosures of this kind are traditionally called hillforts but many of them are very small; Highdown encloses one hectare, and there is no evidence to show that they were ever used as forts. In common with the majority of these hillforts, there has been very little archaeological investigation of the interior of the fort and we really do not know what they were used for. It is sometimes thought that they were small defended farmsteads rather than forts.

Cissbury is one of the best-known and largest hillforts in southern England, with strong defences enclosing 20 hectares (65 acres) following the natural contours of the hill. Its highest point is 184 metres above sea level and gives stunning views extending to Chichester and the Isle of Wight. It was built c.250 B.C. The construction of the fortifications must have taken a colossal amount of co-operative work and illustrates how highly organised Iron-Age society had become. The ditch was originally about 3.5 metres deep, from which thousands of tons of chalk were removed and used to make a bank, parallel with the ditch. The timber revetment which supported the bank is estimated to have used 8-12,000 timbers, each 4.6 metres long and about 18 centimetres in diameter. There were two gateways through the ramparts, at the south and east. There has been virtually no

8 Aerial view of Cissbury showing the Iron-Age ramparts with two entrances. The south-western part of the interior is covered by the lumpy remains of the flint mines.

archaeological investigation of the interior of the fort and its use and function remain a tantalising mystery. A survey by the Royal Commission for Historic Monuments for England in 1993 produced a new plan of the interior, showing large numbers of features. They were created over a long time and have been provisionally dated to between the New Stone Age and the Romano-British periods. Since no evidence has yet been found to suggest that Cissbury was ever used defensively, large-scale investigation of the interior would be fascinating.

In the 1920s, when Findon Valley was being developed, houses encroached further and further up the western slopes of Cissbury. To stop this there was a public appeal co-ordinated by Ellen Chapman and launched in 1921. Cissbury was bought by public subscription for £2,000 and given to the National Trust in 1925 so that it would be safeguarded in perpetuity. Its

surroundings were again threatened by housing developments in the 1950s but these were limited thanks to public demand and the land bordering the uppermost row of houses in Findon Valley is subject to a covenant that prevents further building.

The successful Roman invasion of Britain came in A.D.43, during the reign of the Emperor Claudius. While the debate over whether part, or even all the invasion force came through Fishbourne rather than Kent will no doubt continue for years, what is clear is that the incorporation of southern Britain into the Roman Empire affected all the population to a greater or lesser extent and brought fundamental changes to how society was organised. By the end of the Iron Age the Worthing area was within that occupied by a tribe called the Atrebates. Judging by the palace that was built at Fishbourne near Chichester in A.D.70, possibly for the client king

9 Cissbury hillfort seen from High Salvington on the opposite side of Findon Valley in about 1900. The view is very different today due to all the building that has taken place along Findon Valley.

Togidubnus, and the number of early villas which were built along the coastal plain, it is thought that people in this area were more receptive to Roman ideas and ways than elsewhere in the country. Because of this the transition to Roman rule may have been less traumatic for the local people than for some others.

The coastal plain with its fertile brickearth was popular with the Romano-British population and many stray finds have been made around Worthing as well as several more significant sites. In 1901 part of a Roman milestone was found in the grounds of Herschel Lodge in Grand Avenue. Finds of tile, potsherds and part of a quern were also made which suggest the presence of a small farm in the area. The milestone

is taken to suggest the presence of an otherwise unrecorded Roman road running through Worthing. The milestone has been dated to A.D.308-37, the reign of the Emperor Constantine I. The inscription reads:

DIVI
CONSTANT
P II AVG
FILIO

This translates as 'Son of the divine (or dead) Emperor Constantius'. Constantius was Constantine's father.

A number of sites around Worthing show that there were, at least, a number of farms in the area during the Roman period. When the Museum and Library were being built in

10 This carved limestone head of a Roman boy dates to the second century. It was found in Worthing in the early 20th century but the exact findspot is unknown.

May 1907 the site foreman, Mr. A. Hutton, wrote to the *Worthing Gazette* to say that he and his workmen had found a Roman urn containing burnt bones as well as two other pots. Over the next 12 months several more discoveries were made including pieces of pottery, tile, water pipe and the remains of a wooden box. The newspaper reported that the finds had been handed over to the Museum. Unfortunately the Museum's record keeping at that time was very poor. One of the pots was returned to the Museum in 1950 by a lady in Glasgow. The others remained un-identified until 1997 when a lady in Nuneaton

sent the Museum two postcards, one of which showed the workmen holding the pots at the time of their discovery and the other simply showed the pots. These pictures were so clear that, for the first time, museum staff were able to identify the pots which had been found under their building. A few of the finds are still missing and may have been given away by workmen in the same way as the pot which ended up in Glasgow had been. Other Roman finds have been made around the Museum over the years and it has been suggested that there was a farm on the site. The Museum sits on a small ridge of land

11 Foreman builder Mr. A. Hutton and his colleagues in one of the foundation trenches they dug while building the Museum and Art Gallery. They are holding two of the Roman pots which they had found on the site.

which is the highest point in central Worthing and would, therefore, have been a sensible place for a farm to be built.

In 1845, when the railway was being laid just to the west of Ham Bridge, workmen found 25-30 cremation urns. They also found over 200 nails laid in a circle and some pieces of wood which were interpreted as the remains of a shield. Three weeks later they found more pots, both locally made and imported Samian wares, bones and pieces of glass. The finds were in groups set a few feet apart, with several empty pots set around the one containing the cremated bones. In 1881, a little further to the east, workmen digging in a nursery found a number of similar pots which were dated to the second century.

Traces of Roman occupation have been found on various parts of Highdown Hill, but the most exciting and important discovery was made on the western slopes of the hill in the summer of 1936

and was investigated further by the Worthing Archaeological Society in 1937 and 1938. Further excavation was prevented by the outbreak of the Second World War and has never been resumed. What the excavators originally thought was a small farm turned out to be a bath-house. The cold room, two hot rooms and furnaces were excavated. The walls had been plastered and pieces of mosaic floor and window glass were found. Pieces of datable pottery and a few coins suggest that the bath-house was built in the late first century and went out of use in the late third century. Since it is most unlikely that the bath-house stood by itself on the Downs, there must have been a villa there too, which is still waiting to be uncovered. Other villas have been found along the Downs and coastal strip at Bignor, Angmering, Northbrook College Goring and Southwick.

During excavations in advance of development in Ringmer Road in 1957, three sides of a

12 View of the hot room of the Romano-British bath-house which was excavated on Highdown just before the outbreak of the Second World War. The rest of the villa which must be nearby has never been excavated. The piles of tiles are from the under-floor heating system or hypocaust.

number of rectangular fields were uncovered. They contained a large number of pieces of pottery which have been dated to the first and second centuries A.D. The pottery includes pieces of red Samian ware and a base stamped with the name of the potter, GNATIVS, who was working in Central Gaul in the latter part of the second century. The discovery of fragments of window glass and tiles suggests that there was a substantial building in the area.

The Mill Road hoard of over 2,000 'barbarous radiates' dating to the late third century A.D. was found in half a pot in a sewer trench by council workmen. Their previous trench had cut the pot in two and presumably scattered part of hoard. Barbarous radiates were copies of Roman coins which were made in large numbers and circulated widely at the time. Many of them were very crude. In February 1907 the Goring Hoard, which consisted of about 500 third-century copies of silver coins called *Antoniniani*, was found in a similar but smaller pot in Courtlands brickfield.

During the 1980s, on the Goring site of Northbrook College, the remains of a villa and bath-house were uncovered. The bath-house, across the farmyard from the original villa, has two main rooms and a plunge bath. It now lies under the main College buildings. Further investigations around the site produced Iron-Age pottery. If the site is developed in the future additional discoveries will inevitably be made.

Two

Saxon Worthing to 1750

Towards the end of the fourth century the Romans were having increasing problems controlling various parts of their empire. Britain was attacked by raiders from the Netherlands and Germany, the Angles and Saxons. In the early fifth century some of these groups seem to have

13 This delicate glass flask was found in a pagan Saxon grave in Highdown cemetery in 1892. It was probably made in Egypt in *c*.400. It is inscribed with a scene showing a dog chasing two hares and a Greek inscription which means 'Use Me and Good Health to You'. Even though it was obviously an expensive item its base is uneven and makes the flask lean slightly to one side.

been employed as mercenaries who settled here, perhaps being given land in return for keeping other invaders out. Whatever the policy, increasing numbers of foreigners arrived and settled here. Highdown is the earliest known Saxon cemetery in Sussex, having been in use from the middle of the fifth century. It has been suggested that up to ten of the graves were those of the local Romano-British population, perhaps those who lived in the villa on the western slope of the hill and who employed a group of mercenaries who in turn came to control the area.

The cemetery was discovered in 1891 when the landowner was having holes dug within the prehistoric enclosure so that he could plant a clump of trees. Highdown Hill is the most southerly spur of the South Downs in this area and the clump of trees was to serve as a landmark for sailors for almost a hundred years. The workmen began to dig up pots and jewellery and Mr. Henty contacted the British Museum. Excavation of a large number of graves was then carried out by Charles Hercules Read. Since the cemetery dated to the fifth to seventh centuries the people buried there were not Christians and were buried with some of their possessions. The contents of the graves reflect their relative wealth. Mr. Henty then planted his trees, most of which were blown down in the 1987 storm thus giving archaeologists the chance to carry out a further excavation in the cemetery.

The finds from both excavations are in Worthing Museum and show that at least some members of the community had military links and that others were wealthy. Buckles include types which are usually associated with military graves in the Saxon homelands. Jewellery includes beads of glass or Baltic amber; brooches with elaborate gold decoration inset with garnets; tweezers and fingernail cleaners hung from bronze loops. Knives, spears and shield bosses illustrate the readiness to fight of the men in the community and the wealth is illustrated by pieces of incredibly delicate imported glass. The finest of these has almost no parallel. It is a flask in pale greenish glass with an uneven base. It is decorated with an engraved scene of a hunting dog chasing two hares and a Greek inscription which can be translated to read 'Use me and good health to you'. It has been dated to about A.D.400 and is thought to have been made in Egypt, perhaps Alexandria, and brought to England. It must have been a prized possession before being buried with its owner.

The location of the settlement whose people are buried at Highdown has not yet been identified. Many of the nearby villages, such as Goring, Ferring, Tarring and Worthing itself, have the Saxon -ing element in their name. This element links a group of people to the person whose name forms the first part of the word. In this way Tarring means the people of Tarra. Specialists used to associate place-names containing the -ing element with the earliest phase of Saxon settlement. However, this is no longer thought to be true and the suggestion is that they may belong to a later phase of settlement, perhaps in the seventh rather than fifth century. Dating settlements closely by the elements in their names is not accurate, especially when no other supporting evidence has been found. The name Broadwater is apparently Saxon in origin since it was recorded as Bradenwaetere in A.D.946-55.

Other tangible Anglo-Saxon remains in Worthing are limited to the recent discovery of a few late Saxon sherds and a posthole in the centre of town when archaeologists were examining sites in North Street and Little High Street in advance of development. In the reigns of the late Saxon Kings Aethelwulf and Cnut (1005-1020) coins were minted which carried the word SITHE, SITHESTEB or SITHMES. Scholars have identified this as Cissbury. There were a number of mints in Sussex at this time

14 The Old Palace in Tarring is one of the oldest buildings left in Worthing. Although it is often said to be linked to Thomas à Becket it was not built until some years after his death. This watercolour painting was done by John Nixon in *c.*1800.

15   This view of Parsonage Row cottages in Tarring was taken in 1895 when demolition had started of the furthest two cottages in the row to make way for Glebe Road. It is possible to see that the furthest gable has been partially removed. The cottages themselves have changed very little although the buildings around them have been modernised repeatedly over the years.

16   This view through the old fig gardens at Tarring shows just how thick the grove used to be.

and it has been suggested that an emergency mint was set up at Cissbury during a fairly short period of political unrest. Movement of mints to within hillforts is known to have happened at this time in Wiltshire and Somerset. The coins in use were silver pennies and were stamped with the name of the moneyer who made them, in this instance Ciolwine, Godwine and Leofwine. No remains have been found on Cissbury to back this theory, but Worthing Museum does have one of the pennies from this mint.

Tarring

West Tarring (usually known locally as Tarring) has long been associated in people's minds with Thomas à Becket although there is no evidence at all to suggest that he ever visited the village. From *c*.491 in the time of King Aethelstan to the Reformation, West Tarring was one of the manors owned by the Archbishops of Canterbury. The Old Palace, sometimes called Becket's Barn, was probably where the steward or bailiff who took care of the manor, lived and held court. It is one of the oldest buildings left in Worthing

with parts dating back to the 13th century. It is also possible that it was one of the places where the Archbishops could stay while travelling around their estates.

The oldest houses remaining in the village are the cottages in the High Street known as Parsonage Row. They were originally part of a longer terrace built in the 15th century that extended further to the south. Two cottages were demolished in 1895 to make way for Glebe Road. The Post Office and number 4, next to it, have been modernised. A well at the back of the Post Office was excavated in the 1960s and produced large quantities of 15th- and 16th-century material, including pieces of leather shoes. It was acquired by the Sussex Archaeological Trust (now the Sussex Archaeological Society) in 1927 and run for years as a small museum. It is still owned by the Society but is now run as a restaurant.

In 1444 the people living in Tarring petitioned King Henry VI for help. They claimed that they and their goods periodically suffered at the hands of foreign aggressors, especially the

17   For a number of years in the 19th to early 20th centuries there was a tearoom in the cottage beside the fig gardens. The cottage is almost hidden by fig trees in this postcard.

18 This view of St Andrew's Church, Tarring was engraved in *c.*1820 by Skelton. Church Farm, beside the church, was the home of the Henty family who farmed Merino sheep there before emigrating to Australia in 1831 and getting sheep farming established over there.

French, while they were away at the nearest market, in Steyning. They asked the King for a charter to allow them to set up their own market as they were 'in terror lest their village should be ransacked and their goods taken'. The King agreed to this request and allowed them and their heirs to hold a market each Saturday providing that it did not interfere with any neighbouring market. In the medieval period they also had the right to hold two fairs a year in the village.

An area in South Street, Tarring was once the site of large fig gardens. Although they have gradually been reduced over the years, in 1861 there were still 120 trees which produced over 2,000 dozen ripe figs a year. Tradition would have us believe that Thomas à Becket was responsible for bringing the trees from Italy and planting them here. There is nothing to substantiate this belief and it is more likely that the original trees were planted for St Richard of Chichester in 1244, the bulk of the orchard having

been planted in 1745 from these old stocks. In the late 19th century, Miss Humphries set up a tearoom serving cream teas at her cottage beside the fig garden and this only closed after the Second World War. Visitors were able to walk along tunnel-like paths among the trees. Most of the fig trees were cut down in 1988 to make room for houses.

St Andrew's Church is first recorded in 1372 and is unusually large for a village of the size of Tarring. This probably reflects its links with the Archbishops of Canterbury. The medieval civil parish of Tarring included both Heene and Durrington. The civil parishes were separated in the 16th century but the ecclesiastical parishes remained joined until the 19th century.

Broadwater
The Teville stream used to run between Broadwater and Worthing. In places the surrounding land was below sea level and flooded regularly.

19 The junction of Broadwater Street West and Broadwater Street East in the centre of the village. The road leading off to the right was the main road to Worthing.

The Teville stream joins the Sompting Brook and was clearly once a tidal inlet. It is presumably from this that Broadwater got its name. The stream runs along much the same line as the modern railway and has been culverted to avoid flooding; it drains into the lake at Brooklands.

Sited at the head of shallow Sompting Brook, the parish of Broadwater used to stretch up as far as Cissbury. When a line of beacons was set up across the country in 1587 to pass the alert in the event of a Spanish invasion, two of the beacons were sited on Cissbury. There were also beacons at Goring, Heene and Worthing. Broadwater, as the largest parish in the area, had roads crossing it in all directions. The road to Littlehampton clearly existed by 1419. A road called Brook Street, on the line of what we now call South Farm Road, was in place by the early 16th century. By 1245 an unlicensed market was being held in Broadwater and by 1312 official permission had been granted for a weekly market

to be held, first on Mondays and later on Saturdays. From the reign of Edward III Broadwater was also entitled to hold a fair. A church was recorded in the Domesday survey of 1086 and it was known as St Mary's by 1456. The first inn was recorded in the village by 1690 but its exact location is unknown. The *Maltster's Arms* was in existence by the late 18th century. By 1700 Broadwater was firmly established, with properties along either side of Broadwater Street. It had begun to shrink by the middle of the 18th century but its fortunes revived with the development of neighbouring Worthing as a resort.

Offington, to the north-west of Broadwater, was separate from it in the medieval period. By about 1282 it was probably the principal village in the area. Offington Manor House, later known as Offington Hall, was recorded from 1357 and a chapel and several other buildings were in existence by c.1450. Offington Manor had a windmill by

20 St Mary's Church, Broadwater. This watercolour by R.H. Nibbs was painted in *c*.1836 and shows the Newel Tower which was attached to the main tower and which was removed in the 1880s. A newel tower held a spiral staircase.

21 This painting of Broadwater Mill and the Miller's Cottage was painted in 1893 and is the earliest view of the Mill in the Museum's collections. Originally built in the early 19th century, the Mill was also known as Ballard's Mill or Cissbury Mill. It stood near the present Mill Plantation on the southern slopes of Cissbury and was demolished in the early 20th century.

1418. By 1780 there was a windmill near the present mill plantation. It was known as Ballard's Mill, Cissbury Mill or Broadwater Mill. It was demolished c.1914. One of the oldest surviving buildings in Worthing is the Old Brewhouse, which was part of the Offington Estate. Parts of it have been dated to the late 12th century.

Durrington

After the Norman Conquest in 1066, Durrington, like the Manor of Broadwater, was granted to Robert le Sauvage and by the time of Domesday it had a church. During the Civil War the church was damaged and eventually fell into ruins. A new church was built in Durrington in 1915. By the 13th century Durrington was known for its production of cider but suffered a recession when beer became the more popular drink during the Tudor period.

Although his name is by no means a household word, the philosopher John Selden

22 Offington Brewhouse was part of the Offington Hall Estate. Although it has since been converted into a house, parts of it date back to c.1150.

23 Lacies Farmhouse was where writer and philosopher John Selden was born in 1584. This view is dated to c.1850. The house was later renamed Selden's Cottage. After a fire in 1959 and a period of decay it was pulled down.

24 A rather naïve view of some old cottages in Goring, painted *c*.1802. The painter manages to convey a good impression of the scene even though he or she had a rather poor idea of how to show perspective.

(1584-1654) was one of the most famous people to come from Worthing. Often called the 'Patriot Scholar', John Selden was born at Lacies Farmhouse, later called Selden's Cottage, in Selden's Way, Salvington. He was baptised in West Tarring church. The cottage suffered a fire in 1959 followed by a period of neglect after which it was declared unfit for habitation and demolished. The Worthing Museum has the wooden board from above the front door which is inscribed with a Latin inscription reputedly written by John Selden at the age of ten. In translation it reads:

> Walk in and welcome, honest friend—repose:
> Thief, get thee gone: to thee I'll not unclose.

Selden entered Oxford at the age of 14 and was a law student at Clifford's Inn by the time he was eighteen. It was there that he met Camden, Ben Jonson and other poets. His research and writings made him look into the history of the nation, its

honours, institutions, customs, tithes, etc. He was outspoken in his rejection of the divine right of kings and was sent to the Tower by James I. When he was released he entered Parliament, but he spoke out against the autocratic lawlessness of Charles I and was again sent to the Tower. After eight months he was offered his liberty in exchange for his silence. Refusing the offer he stayed a prisoner for a further two years and was then released on bail. During the trial and execution of Charles I and Cromwell's rise to power he commented that 'the wisest way for men in these times is to say nothing'. After he died he was buried in the Temple Church in London. He left his collection of books to the Bodleian Library in Oxford.

Goring
Recorded as Garinges in Domesday Book, Goring then consisted of four manors. The right

25 Because Sussex lacks good building stone the majority of surviving medieval buildings, like these cottages in Goring, were built of flint and had a thatched roof.

26 Heene Farm and Chapel Ruins painted in 1841 by W.E. Partridge. Heene Chapel was probably there by the time of Domesday Book in 1086. It fell into disuse and by 1778 most of the building had been demolished. St Botolph's Church was built on the site in 1873 and all that remains of the earlier chapel are two pieces of masonry. The farm was one of the largest in the area.

27 A mill at Heind, presumably Heene, appears on the Armada map of the Sussex coast dated 1587. This painting was done in 1890 only 13 years before the mill was pulled down. It stood where numbers 33-7 Mill Road were later built.

28 This map by Robert Morden from 1695 is the oldest showing Worthing spelt (almost) as it still is today. It also includes small pictures of Highdown and Broadwater Mills.

to hold a market on Fridays was granted in 1301. The first church was built 1290-1320 and the chancel was rebuilt in 1380. Records in the church show that, in 1721, 35 people in Goring died of the Black Death. Field Place was built in *c.*1400. Inside the house 17th-century panelling remains although the façade was remodelled *c.*1800.

During six years in the early 17th century James Graves from Tarring and William Cooke from East Grinstead took all the houses in Heene into their own hands. They then turned out all the inhabitants, demolished the houses and dug up the orchards. Needless to say this caused great trouble and hardship and rapidly led to an investigation by the Court of Star Chamber. The Court concluded that Graves and Cooke did own the land and confirmed the displacement of the inhabitants. Graves and Cooke had plans to redevelop Heene but nothing came of them and Heene languished for years. A hundred years later it only had 101 inhabitants, two farms and a windmill. The windmill was in existence by *c.*1600 and was demolished in 1916. The site where it stood is now buried under houses. In the 17th century it was recorded as Heene in Tarring. Heene Chapel fell into disrepair and in 1766 a faculty was granted for its demolition, no

service having been held there for many years—the last having been held by an insane member of the legal profession.

Worthing

Worthing consisted of two manors at the time of Domesday Book and both were granted to William de Braose. The two manors were called Ordinges and Mordinges. The name of Worthing first appeared on a map by Robert Morden dated 1695. By 1724 there were only 60 families in Broadwater and Worthing combined. Worthing remained very small until the fashion for sea-bathing lifted it from obscurity in the second half of the 18th century. By the late 16th century there seems to have been a shingle bar offshore which caused silting; in 1587 lagoons were recorded east and west of Worthing. A large mass of land later called the Saltgrass or Worthing Common gradually developed south of the modern shoreline from the end of the century. During the 18th century the sea eroded this area severely. By *c.*1810 most of the Common land had gone leaving a good beach. As the shingle bar drew closer to the beach it caused a backwater to form which in turn led to complaints from local residents. The shingle bar had been removed at considerable expense by 1802.

Three

The Royal Seal of Approval, 1750-1850

❖

John Olliver (born in 1709) was the last miller at the mill that had stood for several hundred years in the south-west corner of the prehistoric enclosure on Highdown Hill. He was, unquestionably, its most eccentric miller and because of this, and the natural beauty of the spot, his grave became a popular spot for sightseers shortly after his death, and has remained so ever since. Olliver, his wife

29 Pictures of John Olliver's mill on Highdown Hill are almost unknown. This one by J.P.Neale dates to 1818, only a few years before the mill was pulled down. The notes on the picture show that it was a sketch for a painting.

and two daughters lived in a cottage to the north-east of the hilltop. Delighting in the location Olliver built himself a summerhouse where he used to sit and gaze out over the coast. The summerhouse has long since been demolished but it was apparently decorated with some of the miller's many verses. Besides being a miller and poet, Olliver was also an inventor and made his coffin many years before his death. It ran on wheels and was linked to a spring mechanism with which, as he delighted to show visitors, he could make the coffin disappear at the touch of a lever. He built a model of a customs' officer and an old lady which were said to be very life-like and were linked to the mill. When the sails of the mill turned the old lady beat the customs' officer over the head with a broom. Another of his models showed a mill with a miller filling a sack.

Apart from having his coffin ready years before his death and, according to legend, used as a store for smuggled liquor, Olliver also built his tomb 27 years before he died. The landowner, William Richardson, gave Olliver permission to be buried on the hilltop and one of the verses inscribed on the tomb acknowledges this generosity. Olliver died in 1793. According to local legend he was buried upside down so that when the world was turned upside down on the Day of Judgement he would be the only person who met his Maker standing upright. At his funeral his coffin was drawn to the tomb by young women dressed in white robes. One of them was his granddaughter, Ann Street, and she read the sermon. She had been in the habit of sitting and reading to him during his last years when his eyesight was very poor.

Stories of Olliver's links with smugglers have no doubt contributed to the popularity of his tomb. The site was well established as a destination for both locals and visitors to the area by 1805 when John Evans wrote his guide to Worthing and the

THE ROYAL SEAL OF APPROVAL, 1750-1850

30 This painting of 'The Miller's Tomb on Highdown seen from his Summerhouse' by James Rouse in 1823 shows just what a beautiful view he had, the inspiration for his poems.

31 John Olliver, the eccentric miller of Highdown, lived in a cottage to the north of his tomb. It has long since been demolished. This unusual picture of it was painted in 1819 by G.W.A.

32   The view from beside the Miller's Tomb at Highdown painted by William Challen in 1870 shows how empty the landscape was at that time. The few visible landmarks included St Andrew's Church, Tarring.

33   Montague Place, painted by Jacob Spornberg in 1807. This view, looking towards the sea, shows the terrace on the western side which is thought to have held the first lodging houses in Worthing. It is hard to imagine this peaceful scene when standing in bustling Montague Place today.

34 The coloured engraving which formed the frontispiece of Evans' 1805 Guide to Worthing shows Colonnade House on the eastern end of Warwick Street and Warwick House enclosed by trees. The trees were cut down at the start of the 20th century after the Broadway was built.

surrounding area. He described the tomb with all its inscriptions, the cottage and the summerhouse at some length. The mill was demolished in 1826.

The first visitor who is reported to have visited Worthing for the good of his health was a Peter Wycke from London who came in 1759 and stayed at a farmhouse. Between 1750-60, John Luther, another Londoner, clearly recognised Worthing's potential and built the first large house in the area. It was near the southern end of Worthing Street, now known as High Street. Luther was a well-known gambler who is reputed to have lost £100,000 at one throw of the dice but only paid half of his debt. His house was sold by his agents to the Earl of Warwick in 1789 and it was renamed Warwick House. It was soon followed by Sumner House, Montague House and other buildings of note.

The year of 1798 was an important one in the history of Worthing as a seaside resort since it was in August of that year that it gained the royal seal of approval. Amelia, George III's youngest daughter, was unwell and her doctors suggested that a course of sea bathing might help. Worthing was selected because it was not too far from Windsor or Brighton. The King did not want her to go to Brighton itself where her brother, the future Prince Regent, held court in

the Pavilion, and yet he wanted her to be close enough to Brighton for her brother to visit her. She celebrated her 16th birthday on 7 August, one week after her arrival in Worthing. The town, such as it was, was illuminated in her honour. While she was in Worthing her brother did, indeed, come over to visit her but is said to have been far from impressed by her accommodation in Montague Place. The Princess stayed in Worthing until December.

It is interesting to take a look at how Worthing appeared to the Rev. John Evans from London in 1805. Evans had visited Worthing the previous year, and, remarking on the lack of a guidebook, he set about writing one. He described Worthing's origins, saying that,

> Not many years ago it was an obscure fishing town, consisting of a few miserable huts; the inhabitants of which drew an uncertain subsistence from the ocean. None of these houses (as an old fisherman assured me) exceeded forty shillings a year ... garden to the extent of half an acre, might be bought for ... five gallons of brandy.

By 1805, he wrote, Worthing consisted 'of several rows of houses' of which Montague Place and Bedford Row were the longest. It seems

35 John Nixon painted this view of Worthing seafront from Montague Place to the New Inn in *c*.1800, well before the raised promenade was built. The small building on the left is probably one of the old huts from which fishermen sold their catch. The bottom of South Street is on the right-hand side of the picture.

36 John Evans included this map of the area around Worthing in his 1805 guidebook. It shows just how few roads there were apart from the new turnpike roads north to London, west to Arundel and east to Brighton. By the time his book was republished in 1814 several more major roads were marked.

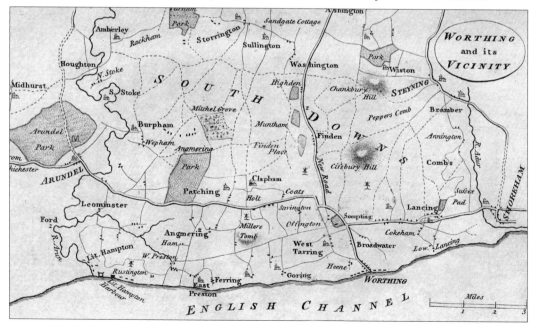

37 The *Sea House Hotel*, later renamed the *Royal Sea House Hotel*, stood on the corner of Marine Parade and South Street. It was built in 1829 to designs by John B. Rebecca. This engraving was drawn by C.W. Wing not long after the hotel opened.

strange today but at that time the Colonnade Library at the western end of Warwick Street gave users an unrivalled view of the sea. The Marine Library on the seafront, run by Mrs. Stafford, was also the Post Office. The post had to come from Brighton as there was no good road to the north and there was one delivery and one collection a day. Evans was but the first of many to extol the virtues of Worthing's warm, sheltered climate and found, to his amazement, that 'Bathers are to be found here at *Christmas*, a circumstance almost exceeding credibility'. In reporting on the facilities which had been introduced to satisfy the visitor's every need, Evans remarked on the fact that two inns close to the beach were run by widows who had taken over the business from their late husbands. Mrs. Hogsflesh was at the *Sea-Hotel* and Mrs. Bacon at the *New Inn*. He described the land between Worthing and Broadwater, adding that it was 'spotted with cattle belonging to the peasantry'.

A second edition of Evans' guidebook, expanded to two volumes and covering more of the surrounding area, was published in 1814. In it

Evans paid tribute to all that the Town Commissioners had achieved in improving drainage, sanitation, and roads as well as establishing a market. He was pleased to note that a Chapel of Ease, the absence of which he had bemoaned in 1805, had been built. He also remarked that there was a Dissenting chapel of moderate size for the convenience of 'those who sincerely and conscientiously dissent from the established church', adding 'That such there are, will not be denied, and they are respectable as well as numerous.'

Within a few years there was quite a range of accommodation available in the town, and soon providing lodgings became one of the town's most important economic activities. The first *Sea House Hotel* may have been on Worthing Common south of Bedford Row in the late 18th century. It was later destroyed by erosion. It was rebuilt by Joseph Parsons from the *Steyne Hotel*, re-opening in 1829. It added Royal to its name after Queen Adelaide stayed there in 1849. It was one of the best hotels in town. Most lodging houses were run by women who were either supplementing their husband's income or who were widows. At the top end of the scale visitors

38 The land where the Steyne was built at the very beginning of the 19th century was earlier known as Singers. When this picture was painted only the terrace along the western side had been built and the ground in front of it had not yet been landscaped.

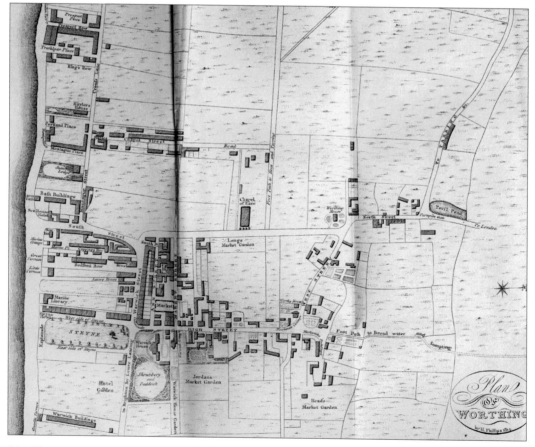

39 The map of Worthing from the 1814 edition of Evans' guidebook shows that the Steyne had been laid out as formal gardens. It also shows just how quickly the town had developed in the 16 years since Princess Amelia brought Worthing to the notice of polite society.

40 This mid-Victorian view of the seafront, looking east, includes several aspects of life in Worthing: fishing boats, a fisherman mending his nets, 'Jerusalem Ponies', bathing machines, lodging houses and people paddling in the sea.

hired a whole house and brought their own servants to wait on them. A cheaper alternative was to hire a suite of rooms or, at the cheapest, to share a room. Many people brought their own food to be cooked by the landlady and her servants but there were so many problems and claims of cheating that soon landladies began providing food themselves. This 'full-board' option was more expensive but less effort. Standards of cooking were often low and caused many a moan. Purpose-built hotels began to appear from the mid-19th century. Private lodgings remained popular. As this work was mostly seasonal people were often short of money in the winter.

Taking the water at inland spas became fashionable in the 17th century. During the following century more and more doctors began promoting the advantages of drinking seawater. A visit to the coast was a cheaper alternative to going to an inland spa. Dr. Richard Russell promoted seawater as a cure-all. He claimed it could cure virtually anything from scurvy, the blue devils or constipation to the effects of sexual over-indulgence. He said it should be drunk in half-pint doses and mixed with milk or port if necessary to make it taste better! Various experts recommended different times of day for bathing and they failed to agree on whether it was better to bathe on an empty stomach or after a light meal. People too delicate to brave the sea could go to the public baths or have seawater taken to their hotel room. For those for whom even this was too much a paddle was suggested, and for the weakest visitors, weeks of walking along the seafront to build up their strength was recommended. After several weeks they might then be strong enough for a paddle. The idea of bathing for the sake of enjoyment came later.

Bathing machines were introduced on Worthing beach as early as 1789 and by 1813 there were sixty. Using a machine cost between 6d. and a shilling including towels. The would-be

32   WORTHING PAST

41 Wicks' original Royal Baths were built by entrepreneur John Wicks in 1797. They were on the seafront near where the Arcade now stands and gave their name to Bath Place. This print was produced by James Rouse in 1817-30.

bather climbed into the machine up on the dry part of the beach. The machine was then pulled into the sea by a horse so that the bather, who had changed into a bathing costume, could slip discreetly into the water. An attendant was on hand to help her take the plunge. In the late 18th century a heavy canvas 'modesty hood' was added to some machines. This was damp and dark and was lowered in front of the machine so that the poor customer could slip into the water unseen. Men did not have to bathe in such miserable conditions. They were often allowed to bathe straight from the beach, albeit not too close to any female bathers. Young men apparently lined up at many resorts with their telescopes trained on female bathers! Ogling bathers was clearly not restricted to men since, a Dr. Granville wrote in the mid-19th century, 'gentlemen bathers drew attention to themselves by standing naked and indecisive on the steps of their machines'. This was presumably for the benefit of women rather then their fellow male bathers.

There has always been debate about the best way to introduce people to swimming. Nowadays

a gentle approach is common, but people were not always so kind. In 1821 one writer attacked the custom of grabbing a yelling child, tipping it over backwards and pushing it under the water. He claimed it was much kinder to duck them face downwards!

Indoor baths were quickly made available for people who were too weak, too shy or simply disinclined to bathe in the sea itself. Mr. Wicks opened his baths in Bath Place in 1797. They were rebuilt in 1833 as the New Parisian Baths. The Royal Baths opened in 1823 in a large, elegant building on the seafront. To the amazement of John Shearsmith, who wrote a guide to Worthing the following year, the baths were very modern and 'steam supersedes almost everything in the shape of manual labour'. It is unlikely that the servants agreed that all manual labour had been done away with! An unusual feature of the Royal Baths was that accommodation could be rented in the same building, allowing even the weakest invalids to take a seawater bath. The types of bath on offer included 'Indian Medicated, Vapour, Shampooing, Hot, Cold, Shower and

42 View looking east from the Signal Station on the seafront in the early 19th century. This is another of James Rouse's prints of Worthing produced between 1817–30.

Douch.' All the baths were made of marble and some had steps going down into them. Those for ladies and gentlemen were on separate floors, each with its own reading or waiting room.

The Esplanade was built in 1820-1. Until then the sea often washed over the front, leaving nowhere pleasant to walk. The Esplanade consisted of a wide public promenade running parallel to the carriage road. It was covered in fine sea gravel and sand that were constantly rolled to keep it smooth. From its position at the top of the beach the people strolling along the Esplanade had a clear view of up to fifty miles along the coast. It was especially popular in the early evening. Shearsmith wrote that, 'at high tide water "plashes" to within yards of the promenader's feet'. At low tide the firm sand was nearly ½ mile wide. Dry and smooth and suitable for horses and people, the sandy beach stretched for thirteen miles from the River Arun to the River Adur. Shearsmith remarked that

there were lots of agates on the beach which women collected.

> It is no uncommon sight to see a fair bevy of the gentle sex, hammer in hand, roaming along the beach, and peering with curious eye among the boulders and shingle in search of these; ever and anon, by a brisk application of the hammer to some promising specimen, affording practical evidence of the invigorating quality of the air, which can brace muscles so tender to such a Herculean task.

He also commented that some other resorts had circulated false, critical stories about Worthing in an attempt to damage its growing reputation.

During the Napoleonic Wars there were a number of invasion threats and from 1790-1812 there were barracks in High Street. A row of Naval Signal Stations was built along the coast. One was built at Worthing in 1795 followed by a Coastguard station after 1809 on the site of the future Esplanade at Splash Point. There was a

43 High Salvington windmill is the only surviving mill in the Borough and has been restored to working order by a band of dedicated volunteers. It is open to the public on alternate Sunday afternoons in the summer.

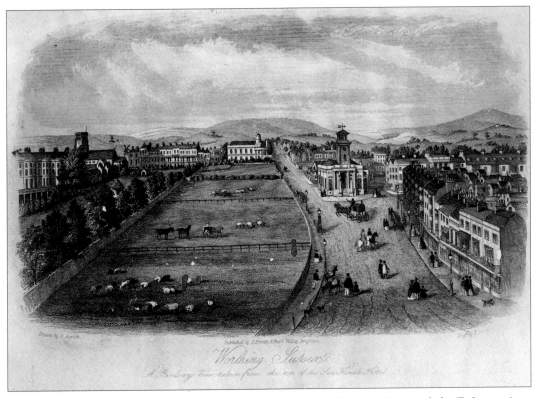

Worthing Sussex

A Railway View taken from the top of the Sea House Hotel

44   This engraved view of South Street from the top of the *Sea House Hotel* was made by T. Jeavons in 1816-17. It shows how much of the western side was still undeveloped at this time. It was owned by the Shelley family and not developed until the 1860s. High Salvington and Broadwater Mills can be seen in the distance.

second one on the border between Heene and Broadwater in the 1820s that remained in use until the 1930s. The Chief Officer's quarters were above the boathouse with cottages for the men and their families at the rear. The third station, at the southern end of Ham Road, was built in 1845 and destroyed by the sea by 1847. Successive buildings were destroyed by the sea in 1850 and 1869 after which there were no more attempts at rebuilding the Signal Station.

Salvington windmill is the last survivor of a group of mills which once served Worthing. Nobody knows when it was built but the earliest map it appears on is dated 1724. It is possible that there were earlier mills in the same area. It was the first mill in England to be insured against fire and a beam still has the seal of the insurance company dated 1774. The first miller whose name is recorded is Daniel Redman in 1824. The mill ceased grinding in 1897 when Charles Davy was the miller. In 1907 the timber roundhouse was replaced

by an octagonal concrete room which was used as a tearoom. It became very popular and old railway carriages were added to the miller's flint accommodation to create more space. The tearoom remained in business until after the Second World War. In 1959 a report by West Sussex County Council suggested that one mill of each type in the County should be preserved. High Salvington was selected to represent a timber-built post-mill and was acquired by Worthing Borough Council. In the 1970s a small group was set up to preserve and restore the mill and to raise money for the restoration. They have done an amazing job and the mill is once again able to grind corn.

Princess Charlotte, daughter of the Prince of Wales, visited Worthing in 1807, arriving with a large escort on 21 July. She stayed at Warwick House and that evening the seafront was illuminated in her honour. While she was staying here she visited her father in Brighton and he came to Worthing to see her.

45   The Old Town Hall in South Street was built on land previously owned by the Shelley family and opened in June 1835. This early 20th-century postcard shows the Midland Bank building on the corner of Warwick Street and a mixture of horse-drawn and motor vehicles.

By the start of the 19th century the resident population had reached around 2,500 and it was clear that many of the town's facilities needed to be upgraded if visitors would continue to be attracted to Worthing. People realised that the first step would be for Worthing to get Town status. An Act of Parliament was passed in 1803 which achieved this. It allowed for the establishment of a group of no fewer than 72 Commissioners to take responsibility for 'paving, lighting, cleaning, watching and improving the streets, passages and places, for establishing an effective police force and purchasing an engine for extinguishing fires'. The Act commented on the poor condition of a number of the streets, lanes and passageways which made up the 'hamlet of Worthing in the parish of Broadwater'. The first meeting of the Commissioners was held in the *Nelson Inn* in South Street. After that they met in the *Royal George Hotel* until the Town Hall was built. They were empowered to raise a rate not exceeding two shillings and sixpence in the pound. In the same Act Cross Lane was established as a public highway and came to be called Montague Street.

In 1809 the Act was amended to allow for the building of a market. It was built between Ann Street and Market Street and opened in 1810. It consisted of a large, paved rectangular area with a pump in the centre and stalls, separated by pillars, round the edges. The two entrances could be closed with large iron gates. Meat, fish, vegetables and fruit were all sold there, as were wheatears and venison when the season was right. Using their new powers the Commissioners employed a one-man police force in the person of Edward Paine. He also served as rate collector and as that invaluable person in the days before television and radio, the town's billposter. This part of his job consisted of going round the town pasting up public notices relating to elections and other events at a specified list of places which included church doors. Billposters even advertised their services in the early street directories.

A fund to raise money for a town clock was started in 1818 but the fund raising was so successful that the Commissioners decided instead to build a town hall. What came later to be known as the Old Town Hall was built in 1834 and

46 View along South Street in *c*.1820 before the western side was developed. The building on the left with a sign above the door is the *Nelson Inn*, where the first meeting of the Town Commissioners took place in 1803.

included a clock tower. It was built beside the junction of Warwick Street and Chapel Road on a plot of land called Wealdens, which belonged to Sir Timothy Shelley. It opened in 1835 and was enlarged in 1847 to provide better space for the courtroom. As well as the Town Hall and Court the building housed the cells in the basement, the fire engine, and apartments occupied by the Superintendent of Police. The Old Town Hall was described, rather unkindly, in the 1891 Ward Locke Guide to Worthing as 'a useful rather than ornamental edifice'. Many people in Worthing were very fond of the building and still mourn its demolition in 1968.

Although Worthing quickly developed a reputation as a good place to visit in winter as well as summer, and was recommended as especially good for invalids, it was hit by the recession which affected many resorts in the 1820s. Times had changed and the earlier custom of spending a long time at the seaside to bathe, take the waters and while away long hours in assembly rooms, libraries and society theatres was no longer fashionable. In about 1828 work had to stop on

the development of Park Crescent, designed by Amon Wilds, owing to lack of capital. It was never completed. The recession lasted into the 1840s and caused a pause to any large-scale building in the town. Worthing never again tried to compete with more fashionable and rowdy resorts such as Brighton. Instead it concentrated on catering for quiet family holidays. Worthing's problems were made worse when the Commissioners mismanaged the finances and nearly bankrupted the town. They had also failed to make the necessary investment in providing a decent water supply and proper sewage removal. The poor drains became a threat to health and the sewage was discharged straight into the sea making the sand sloppy and combining with rotting fish and seaweed to create an unbearable stink. The smell reduced the value of many seafront properties and cleared the area when the wind was in the wrong direction.

During the slump in the 1820s some of the richer townspeople recognised the need to do something to help the suffering of the poor by providing free medical care and advice. They

47   The Dispensary in Chapel Road was built in 1845 and enlarged in 1869. It provided free medical care for poor people who were recommended by someone who paid a subscription to cover their costs.

48   It is difficult to recognise this road as the busy A24 leading from the north into Broadwater. When this picture was painted in *c*.1820 mature trees bordered the road on both sides.

49 The Teville Tollgate, shown in this picture by John Nixon, stood near the modern junction of Teville Road and Chapel Road. The windmill which can be seen in the centre of the picture is the Cross Street or Worthing Mill, which was moved bodily to near Seamill Park Crescent in 1881 and renamed Isted's Mill. The tower of St Andrew's Church, Tarring can be seen in the distance.

established the Worthing Dispensary in Ann Street in 1829. One of the leading lights in this founding group was Dr. Frederick Dixon, who was also a well-known geologist. Three doctors each gave an hour of their time free, twice a week, so that the Dispensary could open from 10-11a.m. on every day except Sundays. The cost of drugs was defrayed by subscription. Those who could afford to do so could recommend someone for care. This cost a guinea a year for six patients. By 1844 it had become obvious that the Dispensary was too small and a new one was built in Chapel Road, near the Old Town Hall. It was demolished to make way for the Guildebourne Centre.

At the end of the 18th century Worthing and its neighbouring villages were still relatively cut off from the main roads in the area by marshes, streams and frequent floods. There was only one road from Broadwater to Worthing. It skirted the west side of Broadwater Green and ran down the line of South Farm Road (then Brooksteed

Lane) before fording the Teville stream. It then forked. The eastern fork led along what is now North Street turning south into Worthing Street (now High Street). After 1802 a direct turnpike road from West Grinstead to Worthing opened avoiding the steep route over the Downs from Steyning. A turnpike gate was built at the north end of Worthing near the Teville Pond. The gate was demolished in 1823 after protests led to the stretch of road from Offington Corner to Worthing being disturnpiked.

In 1803 there were only three coaches a week between London and Worthing. By 1804 there was one a day in the holiday season and in 1817 it was just possible for Londoners to make a day trip to Worthing, although the hours spent in a jolting coach would have made this an exhausting undertaking. The first public train service from Shoreham to Worthing ran on 24 November 1845, creating a link all the way from Worthing to London. The following year

50   This picture called 'The Entrance to Worthing', presumably from the west, shows the smoking chimneys of brick kilns in the distance.

51   The first Worthing Station was built of brick and flint in 1845. A larger station was built a little way to the west in 1868. The original station building is still there but is no longer used by the railway.

the London and Croydon and the London and Brighton Railways were amalgamated to form the London, Brighton and South Coast Railway Company. The first day of the service did not go smoothly. All went well, the first train to reach Worthing being greeted by cheering crowds, until

disaster struck at 1p.m. The trains were still running on a single track and men were still working with horses and carts to increase the width of the embankment with a view to adding the second line. One of the horses took fright at the sight of an approaching locomotive and ran across the line. Even though the train was travelling slowly the horse was killed and the engine was partly derailed. Investigating the delay the Brighton Terminus Superintendent and the Resident Engineer set out in another train only to be derailed at the same spot. To complicate matters further, a third train had left Worthing only to arrive at the crash site and find the first locomotive lying on its side on top of the dead horse. Some of the passengers in the second train decided to get out and walk the three miles to Worthing but were picked up part way by the original train now pulled by three horses instead of a locomotive.

The railway was extended to Goring in 1846. All the early trains ran through Brighton on their way to London and used London Bridge as their terminus. In 1879 the curve from Hove to Preston Park opened which allowed the London to

Worthing trains to bypass Brighton. The introduction of the railway cut the journey time from Worthing to London to just over 2 hours and there were 8 or 9 trains an hour each way in the summer. Compared to coach travel the trains were cheap, quick and could carry many more visitors at a time. They had a huge impact on towns like Worthing, introducing the concept of commuting to London from the coast and also bringing huge numbers of day-trippers to the seaside. A goods yard was built near Broadwater Bridge to handle coal, building materials and livestock.

At Worthing Station horse-drawn taxis awaited visitors to carry them to their hotels or to the seafront. The first horse-drawn bus service started in 1841 and more services were quickly added. In the early 19th century there was a weekly packet boat service between Worthing and Dieppe. Sickly visitors could ride in bath chairs pulled by donkeys which were known locally as 'Jerusalem Ponies'. More robust visitors were offered coach trips to nearby beauty spots such as Chanctonbury Ring or Highdown, sailing or rowing boat trips along the coast, and for children there were rides in little carts or a miniature copy of the Coronation coach pulled by

52 A ride on a donkey, known locally as a 'Jerusalem Pony', has long been a popular attraction in seaside resorts.

53 A popular sight on many seafronts in the late 19th and earlier 20th centuries were carts or carriages pulled by goats. This exceptionally fancy Cinderella coach was a fixture on Worthing seafront until the 1920s. The Council issued licences to the people who owned the goats and carriages and made periodic checks on the welfare of the goats.

54   The Theatre Royal was built by Thomas Trotter in 1807, and the road where it stood was named Ann Street in honour of his wife.

goats. This coach, generally called the Cinderella Carriage, is now said to be in a museum in Paris. It remained popular until around the time of the First World War.

Until the middle of the 20th century there was a fish market on the seafront just to the east of the Pier. Some men used fishing to supplement their income from other occupations such as agriculture. In the 18th and 19th centuries fishing from Worthing Beach was on a large scale and in 1773 John Wilkes apparently came to see 'a great fishery at Worthing'. Mackerel were the main catch in spring and herring in autumn. Oysters were gathered from a bed discovered in 1823-4 a couple of miles off the coast. Lobster, shrimps and crabs and the other fish were all sold by Dutch Auction then sent to London in baskets

known as pads. Although fishing has diminished in scale over the years it is still important in Worthing and some people travel from as far as Surrey at weekends to buy their fresh fish from the fishermen's stands along the seafront.

Some of the earliest theatrical performances in Worthing were staged by Thomas Trotter in a barn at the top of what is now High Street. There was demand for a proper theatre in the town and, in 1803, 34 of the more powerful local people signed a petition appealing for a permanent theatre to be established in the town and suggesting that Thomas Trotter should be employed to run it. In due course the new Theatre Royal was built on the northern side of Ann Street. It opened in 1807 and is sometimes referred to as the Ann Street Theatre. The first

55 Omega Cottage was built next to the Theatre Royal in Ann Street as the home of Thomas Trotter and his wife. It was demolished in 1970 but the delightful little octagonal library was taken apart and rebuilt in Worthing Museum where it is used to display fashion accessories.

performance was a double bill of *The Merchant of Venice* and *Babes in the Wood*. The first season ran for 60 nights. Although Trotter had interests in other towns too, he made Worthing his base and built Omega Cottage in Ann Street as his home. When the cottage was demolished in 1970 the octagonal library was transferred to Worthing Museum. As well as being responsible for the first theatre in Worthing he also built the Royal Baths on the seafront. After 19 years Trotter decided to sell the theatre but instead, in 1826, let it to Evans and Burton. The theatre's fortunes then began to go downhill. The problem was widespread and by no means unique to Worthing. Apart from the occasional performance, the Theatre Royal was closed from 1838 until after Trotter's death in 1851. Under a deal with Trotter's widow and executors Edward Snewin set about refurbishing and re-opening the theatre and for the next few years a wide range of entertainment was presented there. The Theatre closed for the last time in 1855. Having served as a warehouse for Potter and Bailey's grocery business until 1965, the building was sadly demolished in 1970 to make way for the Guildebourne development.

Some of Worthing's delicate visitors found the walk to Broadwater to attend church was too much for them. In 1809 an Act of Parliament was passed which authorised the building of a Chapel of Ease with Broadwater as the parent church. The Reverend Peter Wood, Rector of Broadwater, and 14 trustees were appointed to oversee the project. Funds were raised by public subscription and St Paul's was built fronting land already earmarked for a new road from South Street to the west end of North Street which came to be known as Chapel Road. The Chapel was designed by John Rebecca and completed in 1812 with the Reverend W.M. Davison as the first Chaplain. The costs of paying Davison and maintaining the building were raised by the sale or leasing of the pews. Pew proprietors also had to pay a rate. The original pew proprietors were mostly lodging house keepers who leased them for their visitors. Until the 1880s the pews could be freely bought or sold. In recent years the roof has become unsafe and services are no longer held in the Chapel.

This part of the Sussex coast has a long connection with smugglers and tales of smuggling and smugglers' tunnels abound. Between 1817-31 the Royal Navy ran a Coastal Blockade for the Prevention of Smuggling. In 1827 Lieutenant Henry Leworthy went into action around 10p.m. on 27 March when he and his men met a large gang near Tarring Road. About thirty armed men and up to two hundred others, many with bludgeons, were gathering for a landing and

56 Ann Street before most of these buildings were pulled down to make way for the Guildebourne Centre. The Theatre Royal can still be seen, but by the time this picture was taken it was being used as a warehouse for Potter, Bailey's grocery business.

the appearance of the Blockade Party brought a volley of shots from the smugglers. Men from another Blockade Station then arrived and firing was exchanged for about five minutes. The smugglers then scattered and 39 were reported to have taken refuge in the *George and Dragon Inn* in Tarring. Leworthy placed a cordon round the inn and rode to a magistrate's home to get a warrant to enter the inn. The magistrate was not there so Leworthy had no option but to lift the cordon and let the smugglers escape. In February 1832 a large cargo was due to be landed and a considerable number of men gathered opposite the Steyne to help with the task. A group of

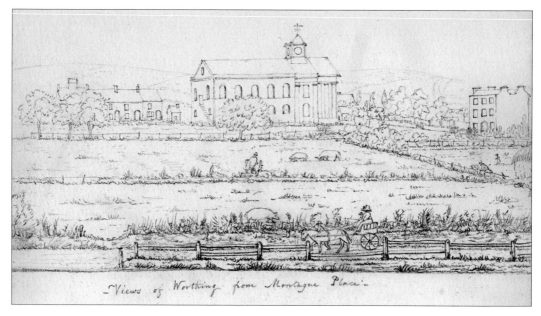

57 A delicate drawing by an unidentified artist of the view from Montague Place to the Chapel of Ease in *c*.1820, about eight years after the Chapel was built.

58 The Chapel of Ease, seen from the north, dominates this picture. It was built on a shallow ridge separated by open land from the buildings that already existed in Worthing. It was designed by J.B. Rebecca and built by Ambrose Cartwright who gave his name to the adjacent Ambrose Place.

Excise men caught them red-handed and there was a running fight as the men fled to Broadwater. One of the smugglers, William Cowerson, was shot dead near the north end of High Street. He is buried in Steyning. After this run-in soldiers were stationed in Worthing to maintain law and order

Early guidebooks have little to say about the villages which were later engulfed by Worthing. Evans and Shearsmith could find little remarkable about Goring beyond the fact that the church had a steeple. At the time they were writing, development had not started in Heene which, in 1800, consisted only of a few cottages along Heene Lane (now Heene Road). The Chapel had fallen into disuse and much of its stone had been removed to be used elsewhere. The majority of the remains were demolished in the 1840s and only a few fragments of wall remain today. In the space of less than fifty years the fashion for visiting the coast had made a town out of a small hamlet, letting Worthing overtake the surrounding villages which had previously exceeded it both in size and importance.

59 This picture of the interior of the Chapel of Ease, by now renamed St Paul's Church, was taken on a glass photographic plate at the end of the 19th century. The photographer was Edward C. Patching, the second Mayor of the Borough of Worthing in 1892-3.

60   Thought to have been painted somewhere on Hill Barn Lane, this picture dated 1841 gives a clear impression of how open and spacious Worthing still was at the time.

61   This panoramic view of Worthing must pre-date 1835, when the first Town Hall was built in South Street. It shows how most of the prime building plots were those which faced the sea.

Four

'The Most Innocent Spot on the Whole South Coast', 1850-90

By the 1850s it was clear that both the town's drainage and its water supply, collected from springs and wells, were totally inadequate for the demands being made of them. Most sewage was still drained straight into the sea through open drains. The 1850 Report of the General Board of Health in the Town of Worthing said that 'the smell of the seaweed when it piles up is nothing like as bad as the smell of the sand at the end of the troughs which carry the town's drainage to the sea'. It also reported that the large cesspools that had been sunk into the beach were very offensive. In 1852 the old Town Commissioners were superseded by a Local Board, elected in accordance with the Public Health Act of 1848.

The first Local Board consisted of nine members, each of whom was elected to serve for three years, although this was increased to 15 in 1867. There was some public opposition to this change but the new smaller Board was much more manageable than the old Commissioners had been and it set to work with a will to improve the town's water supply and drainage. The new waterworks at the north end of High Street was designed by Rawlinson who later designed the Pier. It had three wells from which water was pumped to a water tower which held 110,000 gallons. The waterworks closed in 1896. As well as dealing with the water supply and sewage the Board had wide responsibilities including public works,

62   The first modern waterworks in Worthing were designed by Robert Rawlinson and built in 1853-7 at a cost of £30,000. They stood at the north end of High Street and stand out clearly in late 19th-century panoramas of Worthing as the tallest buildings in town. The waterworks were demolished in 1924.

63 The *Marine Hotel* is on the right and the *Sea House Hotel* on the left in this mid-19th-century view looking up South Street from the seafront. By this time it had become one of the main shopping streets in Worthing.

groynes, paving, lighting, street cleansing, licensing hackney carriages, bathing machines, etc. and raising and disbursing rates.

Visitor numbers went up steadily and Worthing's reputation as a town which was good for invalids grew. The Downs gave it shelter from cold north winds so that it was rightly known for its even, warm climate. By 1865 the winter season was growing in importance. One writer in the *Daily Telegraph* in August 1873,

quoted by Lower in his guidebook, recommended Worthing as somewhere to relax between enduring the rigours of the races at Brighton and Goodwood. He described Worthing as 'an oasis in the desert of sin … the most innocent spot on the whole south coast of England. For Worthing is almost wholly given up to children and domestic joys … Worthing is profoundly happy … She envies neither Brighton nor Bognor.' Throughout this period the area around South Street and Warwick Street were the commercial and administrative centre of the town. Here, all the largest shops could be found as well as the first banks. In time shops spread along Montague Street and up Chapel Road but the junction of South Street, Chapel Road, Warwick Street and Liverpool Road remained the heart of the town with the Old Town Hall the focus for numerous celebrations.

Worthing's position as a centre for market gardening and glasshouses started in the 1850s, and it was apparently a doctor who was the first grower to sell his produce. The first glasshouses we know of were in Broadwater, where C.A. Elliott is said to have grown grapes under glass which came from the Great Exhibition, and the glass houses soon spread to Heene, west of Grand Avenue. One of the most

64 An unrecognisable view of Warwick Street in *c*.1850, seen from the east, with the railings of Steyne Gardens in the foreground. It shows what a wide, elegant street it was designed to be and how attractive the buildings on the north side were before modern shop-fronts were added.

65 The vines in this greenhouse seem to be producing a heavy crop. It is interesting to note that the tallest vines are only just above the standing man's head. This must have been to make harvesting them easier. The men appear to be removing surplus leaves from the vines.

popular fertilisers in the early days was fish. Piles of surplus sprats were dumped beside the glasshouses, the workers were allowed to take some home for their breakfast and the rest were allowed to rot until they had decayed. They were then dug into the soil. The soil along the coastal plain had long been know for its fertility, but it was the coming of the railway that allowed the industry to grow so fast, enabling produce to be transported to markets in London. Some of the grapes were exported to America and France. In 1905 a new goods yard was built at West Worthing station to specialise in handling this produce. The main crops were grapes, tomatoes and cucumbers interspersed with chrysanthemums in winter. Large numbers of people were employed in the glasshouses and in packing the produce. In the 1930s Worthing had 250 growers employing 1,500 workers. Sadly the growing population

66 The main flower crop grown around Worthing was chrysanthemums. These men are busy harvesting the flowers ready to be sent to markets in London and elsewhere.

increased the demand for building land and this led to a decline in the glasshouse industry. By the 1970s the glasshouses had all but gone from the Borough.

67 Page's Nursery in Ham Road was founded in 1887. It grew grapes and tomatoes in summer and flowers in winter. This picture shows one of the glasshouses shortly before it was pulled down in 1968.

68 Christchurch was built in 1843 as a second Chapel of Ease and was paid for by public subscription. It was made a parish church in 1855. It was said to have been built in response to a demand from poorer people for somewhere in Worthing they could worship.

The parish of Broadwater was divided to create the parish of Christchurch in 1855, and St George's was added in 1867, Holy Trinity in 1884, St Andrew's in 1888 and St Paul's acquired its own parish in 1892. The need for so many new churches illustrates the speed with which the population was growing. Services for Roman Catholics were held at Offington Hall Chapel, owned by Thomas Gaisford, from 1859. Later, St Mary of the Angels and Sion Convent were built on land owned by Gaisford in Richmond Road. Nonconformist worshippers

69   A view from Broadwater church looking north and showing large areas covered by glasshouses.

70 The Wesleyan Chapel in Bedford Row opened in 1840 and seated 520. The Minister changed every three years and held three services a week. When the Steyne Gardens Methodist Church replaced it in 1900 the Bedford Row Chapel was converted into Bedford Hall and used as an auction room.

were catered for by a range of chapels throughout the town.

Worthing has never been known as a town which was quick to adopt new ideas and yet it was only the 13th in the country to build a pier. The idea behind piers was to provide a way for people to go out over the sea without risk of being shipwrecked or seasick. The Worthing Pier Company Limited was set up in 1860 to finance and build a pier in the town. It used 6,000 £1 shares to raise the money and on 4 July 1861 the first pile of the new pier was sunk into the seabed off the end of South Street. It was designed by Sir Robert Rawlinson and officially opened to the public on 12 April 1862. This first pier consisted of wooden decking 5 metres wide and 295 metres long standing above the water on an elegant iron framework. There was a small tollhouse at the landward end. The first Piermaster was a 52-year-old former coastguardman, Henry Hayden.

The Pier was an instant success and the Pier Company decided to expand it. In 1884 two kiosks were added by the entrance. One housed the tollhouse and the other sold souvenirs. In 1888 the Pier Company raised another £20,000 through 40,000 ten shilling shares so that they could double the width of the decking and add an entertainment pavilion at the southern end of the pier. On the day of the re-opening 7,000 people paid the toll to go on the Pier. In 1890 the toll was one penny, which was doubled when the band was playing, 3d. was charged for a dog

71 Worthing Pier opened in April 1862 and this watercolour of the view east from the Pier was painted in September of that year.

72 A view of the new Pier from the east. In 1862 piers were still very much a novelty and this was only the 13th to be built. Its simple design accords well with its original function of letting people walk out over the water without fear of getting shipwrecked or seasick.

73 As this photograph from 1880 shows, the original Pier was little more than a wooden deck on an iron frame with a tollhouse at the landward end.

74 By 1889 the first improvements to the Pier had been added. A pavilion had been built at the southern end and two kiosks had replaced the old tollhouse. One kiosk was used to sell tickets and the other, fancy goods. The landing stage at the southern end is clearly visible.

75 The *Worthing Belle* was the last of the 'Shilling Sicker' steamers to provide a regular service along the coast. She was sold to the Turkish Navy and renamed the *Touzla*.

and 4d. for a perambulator, and 6d. for a bathchair (the last two prices included entry for the attendant).

One very important section of the Pier was the landing stage at the southern end. Paddle steamers which carried people on trips along the coast were moored there. These boats were known as 'Shilling Sickers'. The *Worthing Belle* was the best known of them. She was built on the Clyde and originally called the *Diana Vernon*. She was owned by William Reed and ran until 1913 when she was sold to Turkey as a ferry and renamed the *Touzla*. She was scrapped in 1936. The *Waverley* which visits the Pier each summer is the last paddle steamer on the south coast.

In 1863 William Richardson, who was an important local landowner, sold Heene Manor Farm to the Heene Estate Company. They sold

76 This enchanting panorama of Worthing beach and seafront was painted in the 1860s and shows all the grand buildings at their best. It makes the framework under the Pier look very delicate and elegant. It also shows a good range of seaside activities underway, from paddling and rowing a boat to strolling along the beach or working on a fishing boat. The light makes it look as though the painting was done in the early morning.

77 Heene Terrace was completed in 1866. Worthing and Heene were still distinct at this time and Heene Terrace was the main seafront building in Heene for a number of years.

it on to the West Worthing Investment Company which was established with the idea of developing Heene as a town in its own right. A team of Commissioners for West Worthing was set up to administer the area from their offices in 93 Rowlands Road. In 1865 Heene Terrace was completed. The small West Worthing waterworks opened in 1867 and were enlarged in 1884 to supply all of Heene parish, West Tarring and part of Broadwater. A second well was sunk in 1887 and a reservoir was added at Durrington in 1894. During the typhoid epidemic which struck Worthing in 1893 this supply was called on to

78 Heene Baths and Assembly Rooms were built in 1866. They were part of the West Worthing development and were hailed as among the most modern baths in the country. Growing increasingly tatty after a period of inevitable neglect during the Second World War, the Baths were closed in 1968 but not demolished until 1973.

provide safe water for the town centre as well as Heene. The first large houses were built along Heene Road at this time.

The West Worthing or Heene Baths opened in Heene Road in 1866. Built in a Venetian Gothic style, it included a tunnel that led under Heene Terrace to the sea so that fresh seawater could supply the baths at each high tide. A number of guidebooks claimed that they were the finest baths in the country. They offered hot or cold, salt or freshwater baths, a swimming pool and an Assembly Room. A later addition was the fashionable Ozone Baths. In 1875 a roller skating rink opened next to the baths to be followed in 1881 by pleasure grounds and a tennis court in front. The whole complex was demolished in 1973 and is now the site of an office block. The writer in the *Daily Telegraph* in August 1873 gave the baths an enthusiastic review, noting,

> Up in West Worthing some handsome speculators have built some swimming baths, which in point of taste and comfort cannot be excelled, even at sister Brighton. Under that same Gothic roof are offered also that new luxury called an ozone bath, wherein those who require luxurious rest are permitted to doze and dream, reposing the while on a soft couch of oozy seaweed.

Floods caused by especially high tides have always been a problem in Worthing, in spite of all the efforts that have been made to make the sea defences impregnable. One of the worst floods came in 1877 when South Street was flooded up

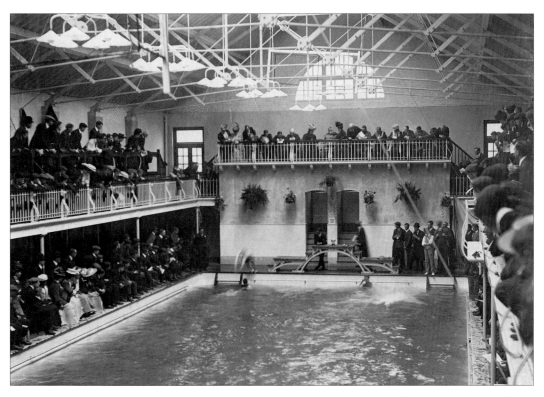

79 Heene Baths were the setting for countless swimming, diving and water polo competitions as well as being used for recreational swimming. This crowd seems to have gathered to watch a swimming race in *c*.1900 and every available seat is full.

to the steps of the Old Town Hall and a number of people took to their boats. Damage to all the shops in South Street must have been appalling and particularly high tides, combined with strong southerly winds, were dreaded by traders and householders alike.

Housing development really got going in the 1870s when Worthing became somewhere to live rather than just visit. Much of this development was in the west, including the Gratwicke Estate. In the east, Homefield Park, then called The People's Park, was laid out around a delightful lake fed by the Teville stream. One section of East Worthing which was developed at this time was called Seldenville. This included the large houses in Farncombe Road and surrounding streets. The seafront remained undeveloped. A boost to the western part of the town came when West

80 Periodic flooding has long been one of the hazards associated with living on the coast. One of the worst floods came in January 1877 and was produced by a combination of gales and high spring tides. The floodwater reached as far as the steps of the Town Hall and, as this picture shows, some people took to boats to travel along South Street.

81 The People's Park, later renamed Homefield Park, was the first municipal park in Worthing and opened in 1880. It was planned around a lake into which the Teville stream drained and was laid out with graceful paths and a rustic bridge.

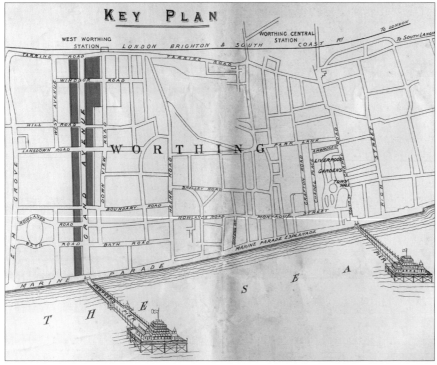

82 This plan was printed on the back of the large brochures which were produced to advertise the delights of the planned development in and around Grand Avenue in the 1880s. It shows that the planned second pier would have looked very like the one in central Worthing.

83 The half-built shell of the *Hotel Metropole* stood at the southern end of Grand Avenue. It was started in 1893 as part of the grandiose plans for making West Worthing into a resort in its own right, but ran into financial difficulties. As this picture shows, there were very few buildings around it and the looming shell was soon nicknamed 'Worthing's White Elephant'.

84 After thirty years the half-built *Hotel Metropole* was completed as a block of flats. Originally called The Towers when it opened in 1923, it was renamed Dolphin Lodge in 1971 when a second block was attached at the corner of Grand Avenue and the seafront.

Worthing Station opened in 1889 but this was not enough to save the grandiose development plans which had been drawn up in 1882. Building plots along a new road called Grand Avenue were laid out as part of this plan which even included a proposal for a second Worthing Pier. Work started on a large building at the southern end of Grand Avenue which was intended to be the *Metropole Hotel*. Sadly, like the elaborate plans for Park Crescent earlier in the century, this development came to a halt due to lack of money. The skeleton

of the Metropole stood guard over the seafront, unfinished, until the 1920s. It was then completed, not as a hotel but as flats called first the Towers and then Dolphin Lodge. In 1890 West Worthing was absorbed into the new Borough of Worthing.

The early years of the fire brigade in Worthing are not fully recorded although, as noted in Chapter 3, providing a fire engine was one of the responsibilities of the Worthing Commissioners. The fire engine in the Museum is thought to have been in use *c.*1830 and was

85 Worthing's regular fire brigade was set up in 1855. Fourteen years later it was renamed the Worthing Volunteer Brigade. A Borough Fire Brigade was set up in 1893, three years after the incorporation of the Borough, and these men were its members.

86 The Borough Fire Brigade performed displays in many of the town's celebrations. This display shows the men up their ladders while a procession passes underneath. The occasion was the coronation of King George V in June 1911. People have climbed onto the outside of the buildings on the right to watch what is going on.

replaced by a larger machine in 1841. It was apparently in the care of one man who used a gong to summon citizens to his aid in fighting fires. In 1869 the Worthing Volunteer Fire Brigade was formed with three centres in East, Central and West Worthing. When Goring Hall was destroyed by fire in 1862 the Worthing horse-drawn machine arrived ten minutes after the alarm was raised. In 1890 the three centres were amalgamated into one brigade which was renamed the Worthing Borough Fire Brigade in 1891. It was staffed by a chief officer, captain, lieutenants, superintendents, firemen and messengers. The principal station, in the Old Town Hall, was completed in 1893 at a cost of £200 for equipment. A new headquarters was built in High Street in 1903 and in 1911 the first motor fire engine was bought.

87 The Chief Constable of Sussex kept an album of newspaper cuttings recording the events surrounding the Salvation Army Riots in Worthing in 1884. When press photographers were not around the newspapers illustrated the dramatic scenes with pen and ink drawings.

88 At the peak of the troubles caused by the conflict between the Salvation and Skeleton Armies the local magistrate, Thomas Wisden, called in the troops from Preston Barracks and read the Riot Act. There was widespread shock that such violent events could have taken place in such a traditionally quiet town.

The Salvation Army was formed by General Booth in 1878 and operated through militant evangelism. They met opposition in many areas, but rarely as fierce as that which erupted in Worthing. In the 1880s local bonfire clubs regularly came into conflict with the police around 5 November, getting drunk and causing fighting in the streets. Rowdy celebration of bonfire night was and remains a feature of Sussex life but it was guaranteed to upset the Salvation Army. A small group of Army members came to Worthing late in 1883 with the avowed aim of fighting Satan, and they targeted the Worthing Excelsior Bonfire Club which met at the *Royal George*, 'Pacey's Blood-hole'.

Local people objected to the idea that they needed the Salvation Army to save their souls. The Army could only operate with police support and the Home Secretary ordered that opposition to the Army in Worthing be stamped out once and for all. But writers in the *Worthing Gazette* were vehemently opposed to the organisation. Until April 1884 the Army was willing to compromise by not parading through the streets, then a new captain, 23-year-old Ada Smith, was appointed and decided that far from staying in their barracks the Army would parade through the streets twice each Sunday to 'attack the devil'. The bonfire boys, under the name of 'The Skeleton Army', tried to impede the parades, singing parodies of the Salvationists hymns and calling them 'Booth's Baa-lambs'. They would get ahead of the Salvationists and, once outside Montague Hall, turn and hurl missiles including soot, eggshells hardened with blue paint, flour and black lead. Local reports blamed the Salvation Army for

the problems and the police did little to curb the actions of the Skeleton Army. Captain Smith said that she was very surprised at the troubles and that 'she did not know there was such sin in Worthing'.

On Sunday 17 August 1884 the rioters were particularly aggressive and on the following day went to the Salvation Army barracks and threw bricks through the windows during their meeting. They also smashed up the shop of Mr. George Head, an ironmonger who belonged to the Salvation Army, and he fired on the intruders. He later appeared at Maidstone Assizes but was acquitted. On 20 August the Skeleton Army took to the streets forming a crowd of three to four thousand. An urgent call to the barracks in Brighton brought the Royal Irish Dragoons, who rode into the crowd in South Street and dispersed it after Colonel Wisden had read the Riot Act at 11.30 p.m. The following Sunday the disruption was carried into the service by women whose husbands were in custody over the earlier riots. There was much anger that some of the men had been fined for their actions. The problems continued for a few months on a smaller scale and by the autumn had begun to simmer down.

According to an article in a magazine called *The Schoolmaster* in September 1884, 'The children of Worthing now amuse themselves by playing at Salvation Army riots. Following the riotous example of their elders they range themselves into Salvationists and Skeletonists, singing parodies of General Booth's hymns.'

Although Sussex suffers from a lack of good building stone it is blessed with abundant amounts of brickearth which is suitable for brick making.

89   The *Steyne Hotel*, which stood at the corner of The Steyne and the seafront, was the first hotel in town. It was where fashionable society gathered for assemblies and balls in the early 19th century. In 1956 it was bought by the neighbouring *Chatsworth Hotel*.

90   The third Lifeboat House was built on the seafront near the Coastguard House in 1874. This postcard was sent in 1908 and shows the *Richard Coleman* and the crew in the entrance to the Lifeboat House. The building still stands but it has an unsightly ground floor extension which spoils its appearance.

Around Worthing some of the brickearth contains enough calcium to allow 'white' as well as red bricks to be made and these were widely used in the late 18th and early 19th centuries. In his 1805 guidebook, John Evans commented on the blue clay which was extracted from the land next to the beach and was used to make cream-coloured bricks. Brickfields and public houses are often found close beside each other and people who owned one often had an interest in the other. One local example of this was the *Half Brick* public house that was close beside the Navarino brickfield in East Worthing. It has also been suggested that when Worthing was developing quickly small brickfields were set up beside each new area of development to supply bricks and that once the building had finished there the brick-makers moved on. Brickfields of this type, using clamp burning, existed in Broadwater, East Worthing, Heene, West Worthing and Durrington. The first records of brickmaking around Worthing date back to the 1770s but it reached a peak in the late 19th century when the town was expanding fast. Heene Terrace and the *Burlington Hotel* are among the important Worthing buildings that are made of local bricks.

In 1850 a trading vessel, the *Lallah Rooke*, got into difficulties in a storm off Worthing and 11 fishermen from the town died attempting to help the stricken boat. Following the disaster, the

91 The first launch of Worthing's third and final lifeboat, the *Richard Coleman*, in August 1901. The boat was named after the donor's late husband and stayed in service until 1930.

Rev. W. Davison of Broadwater organised an appeal to help the families of the victims. A memorial tablet was erected in Broadwater church. At this point Captain Forbes RN from Lancing suggested raising funds to acquire a lifeboat for Worthing. A committee that was set up realised that it needed to fund a lifeboat house and a carriage as well as a lifeboat. The carriage was for transporting the boat from the lifeboat house to where it could be launched. In 1852 a self-righting lifeboat was ordered, even though all the necessary funds had not yet been raised. It arrived for sea trials the following June watched by large crowds on the beach. The crew made several attempts to capsize the boat, but failed each time. It was housed in a purpose-built stone house next to the Signal Station.

The lifeboat crew was made up of local fishermen and other watermen and was financed by local contributions. Admiral William Hargood and later his son, Harry, were always at the forefront of fund raising and support for the lifeboat. In 1865 the RNLI took over the support and control of the Worthing lifeboat and decided to build a new lifeboat station. It was built in Crescent Road, close to the site of the present Salvation Army Citadel. They also ordered a new boat, funded by an anonymous donation and called the *Jane*. She was launched in 1866 and the naming ceremony was performed by Admiral Hargood's wife. The disadvantages of having a Lifeboat House which was not on the seafront were soon obvious and the final lifeboat house was built at 107 Marine Parade with a turret at the front. Although much

92 Thomas Lester became Head Coastguard in Worthing in the late 19th century, serving until 1913. He was a familiar sight patrolling along the seafront to Goring and back.

altered it is still a distinctive feature of the seafront. The boat was launched from the beach east of the pier and horses still pulled it from the house to the launch site. In 1880 the *Jane* was renamed the *Henry Harris*. When it was necessary to launch the boat the men were summoned by means of a maroon which was kept on the foreshore.

In 1887 a new boat, also called the *Henry Harris*, was launched in celebrations which doubled as those for Queen Victoria's Golden Jubilee. Throughout the second half of the 19th century the lifeboat, on its carriage, and with the men in their smart uniforms (used only for special occasions) were a central part of any procession. In 1887 they processed through the town with the Fire Brigade, Temperance Society, Cycle Club and Worthing Brass Band and enjoyed huge crowds. There was a firework display in the evening. The *Richard Coleman* was ordered in 1901, donated by Mrs. Birt-Davies Coleman in memory of her husband. Both boats went through the town in procession. For eighty years the lifeboat, manned by volunteers from the local community, was launched on countless occasions to help sailors and ships in distress. Many lives were saved through their efforts, and in the course of these rescues some Worthing lifeboatmen lost their lives. The last Worthing lifeboat was taken out of service in 1930 to the great regret of the local community.

93 Thomas Lester, his wife and nine children lived in the Coastguard's Cottage on the seafront. It is the low building in the centre of this photograph.

The presence of coastguards in the town remained important. From the late 19th century until 1913 the Head Coastguard was Thomas Lester. He patrolled the coast from Worthing to Goring where he met his counterpart from Ferring and turned back to retrace his steps. He always carried his 'tuckstick', which was a type of swordstick favoured by coastguards, who would stick it into suspect bales and similar items to check they were what they were supposed to be. Thomas Lester lived in the small Coastguard's Cottage on Marine Parade with his wife and nine children.

In 1858 two new wards were added to the Dispensary in Chapel Road but by the late 1870s it was clear that it had outgrown the available space. In 1882 it moved to new premises in Lyndhurst Road which cost £5,000. It still contained only two wards and in 1888 a new children's ward was added. It was renamed Worthing Hospital in 1904, in spite of the opposition of some people who felt that the old name did not need replacing, and continued to have additional facilities tacked onto it over the years. The hospital is still on the same site although expanded and largely rebuilt in the 1990s.

94 A purpose-built infirmary opened in Lyndhurst Road opposite the northern end of the Beach House Estate in 1882. It was renamed Worthing Hospital in 1904. Originally small, it has been expanded and updated a number of times and the Hospital is still on the same site today.

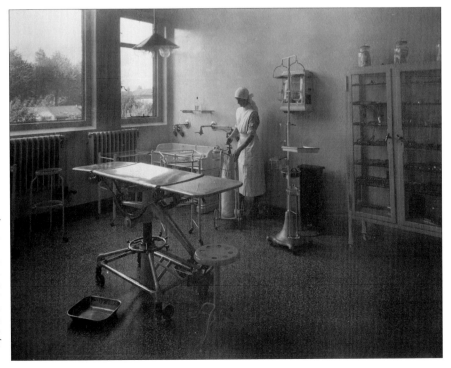

95 An album of photographs was collected to mark the construction of vastly improved facilities at the Hospital in 1921. Although this operating theatre may look horribly basic to modern patients, it was welcomed as a big step forward by the people of Worthing.

96 The parts of this panoramic view of Worthing which deal with the town are accurate, and numerous landmarks including the Pier, Waterworks, *Sea House Hotel* and St Andrew's Church, Tarring can easily be picked out. However, the artist has used considerable licence in his portrayal of the Downs, which look more like a range of mountains than gently rolling hills.

97   Charter Day on 3 September 1890 was an occasion for great celebrations, the day on which the town of Worthing was incorporated as a Borough. It was also the day on which West Worthing was amalgamated with Worthing.

The introduction of fixed Bank Holidays in the late 19th century enabled many more people to make a day trip to the coast and brought a considerable amount of business to Worthing. On Bank Holidays numerous trains plied to and from London and the beach and promenade were buzzing with life. However, some people were not happy to have the seaside opened up in this way, complaining that resorts were getting too crowded.

When a fire broke out in the Colonnade in 1888 it was discovered in the early hours of the morning by a passing policeman, Sergeant Byrne. He blew his whistle to summon a colleague who he then sent to raise the alarm by ringing the fire bell at the Town Hall. Sergeant Byrne set about rescuing the occupants of the building. The fire engine then arrived, but without firemen or even a hose. One of the onlookers, Charles Bridger, who had arrived on the scene without hat, coat or shoes, then rushed off with some other men to fetch a hose from the Town Hall. In the meantime the fire got an ever stronger hold on the

98   The assembled members of the first Council of the Borough of Worthing in 1890. Alfred Cortis is in the centre of this picture wearing the new robes and chain which went with the office of Mayor.

building. Eventually several firemen arrived and got the machine in working order, but they could not agree on where to place it, which caused further delays. Frustrated by this, some of the onlookers raced back to the Town Hall and collected the other engine and began to tackle the fire themselves. The fireman with the main engine had more problems when it became obvious that the hose was in very poor condition and had a number of leaks through which water doused both firemen and onlookers. Frederick Blaker and some helpers began removing furniture, including the piano, from one of the houses but their fumbling and uncoordinated efforts in the dark caused additional damage. At one point a coastguardman climbed onto the roof of an adjacent building, hose in hand, ready to douse any flames which might spread, but there was no water to supply his hose. In the end the Colonnade was completely gutted and if it had not been a

windless night the fire could easily have spread to the whole of Warwick Street. The shell of the Colonnade was strong enough for the houses to be rebuilt but number three was lowered by two storeys and the balcony at the north end was removed.

When Warwick House was vacant in 1886 Mr. H.H. Jordan suggested that the Town should buy it in order to create a Winter Garden. Apparently a lease of 40-100 years was available at a cost of £400p.a. with an option to purchase for £10,000 at any time. For whatever reason, the Council decided not to pursue this idea and a lovely house was lost to the town.

In the months leading up to Queen Victoria's Golden Jubilee in 1887 a writer in the *Worthing Gazette* of 23 March wrote, 'The fact that this is a jubilee year does not add to the income of anyone, and secondly, the town is divided as to the desirability of increasing the number of its residents and tourists.' He urged the town to organise nothing in the way of celebrations. In a true spirit of economy the decision was taken to combine Jubilee celebrations with those marking the arrival of a new lifeboat, as we have already noted.

Alfred Cortis (1833-1912) was a local man who made an indelible mark on the history of Worthing in the run up to its new designation as a Borough. A corn and seed merchant, he not only found time for civic duties but was also a member of the local Volunteer Force and a superb shot, winning prize after prize in national and international competitions. In 1881 he was elected a member of the Local Board of Health, chairing it for the last two and a half years before the inauguration of the Borough. The first election of councillors was held in November 1890. He was elected to represent the Central Ward, and was chosen as one of the Borough's first Aldermen and its very first Mayor. As a mark of recognition for his part in the change from town to borough he was presented with his portrait, painted by the well-known artist Ponsonby Staples in 1892.

The cost of the painting was met by public subscription. He was also one of the first local representatives on the West Sussex County Council, being elected in 1889. Cortis never married and used his resources to give generously, and often anonymously, to a number of local charities, including the Hospital and, as will be seen in the next chapter, the Museum.

The creation of the Borough of Worthing was very important in the development of the town. The Royal Charter of Incorporation was awarded on 3 December 1890 with six aldermen and 18 councillors representing five wards. Heene was amalgamated with Worthing. When the Borough was extended in 1902 this was increased to eight aldermen and 24 councillors. In 1890 the population of the Borough was 16,606. The first Town Clerk was William Verrall, who had previously been clerk to the Local Board. Borough status gave the development of Worthing a new impetus and the Council began to promote it as a place to both live and visit, describing Worthing in its guidebooks as 'The City of Health in the Land of Gardens' and 'Sunny Worthing'.

Five

'Seaside Town of Grape and Fig', 1891-1929

One of the entertainment highlights of 1892 must surely have been the advertised balloon ascent and parachute descent in Beach House Park. Mr. Reginald Paine described what he saw on this occasion to Henry Gooch, watching events from the top of the Old Water Tower. The balloonist took far less money from selling tickets than he had expected and delayed the ascent for a considerable time. Crowds had lined up along the Brighton Road to watch the ascent without paying. After one bright spark climbed over a low wall into the park, by-passing the ticket booth, others quickly followed in large numbers. Mr. Paine ran down from the Tower to join them. The balloonist, seeing the advancing crowd, hurriedly began his ascent. He came down in the sea off the Pier, having kicked off his boots which would otherwise have weighed him down. He was quickly rescued. Mr. Paine was still on his way from the Water Tower to the Park when

99 After the typhoid epidemic which devastated the town a fresh well was sunk on the Downs. A new water main led from the well at Lyons Farm to High Street. This picture of High Street shows the new main being laid.

71

these events occurred and he missed all the excitement.

Worthing's reputation as a healthy resort suffered a devastating blow in 1893 when a typhoid epidemic swept the town. During the early part of the year an unusually high number of people suffered from diarrhoea, but none of them died. By the spring, doctors were becoming concerned. By May, patients suffering from typhoid had filled the few beds available at the Infirmary and were being accommodated in tents outside where stifling heat added to the distress of both patients and staff. As the epidemic progressed various other buildings were taken into use as temporary hospitals. The cause of the infection was traced to contamination of the water supply with sewage. Water carts were placed around the town to provide safe drinking water from the West Worthing Waterworks. In only ten days a water main was laid leading from a newly sunk well at Lyons Farm to High Street. In July there were 1,261 recorded cases and 155 deaths in Worthing. By the end of August there

were said to be no visitors left and Worthing was like a ghost town. As a writer in the *Sussex Daily News* noted, the epidemic caused hardship to the whole town and not just those who were ill. Worthing was, first and foremost, a resort where people came to improve their health, and the majority of the townspeople earned their income by providing services of one kind or another to the visitors. It was estimated that the outbreak cost the London, Brighton and South Coast Railway £15,000 in lost revenue and it took several seasons for visitor numbers to recover. A total of 1,416 people were infected with typhoid and 188 died. In 1897 a new reservoir and pumping station were opened on the Downs north of Broadwater.

During August and September 1894 Worthing had an eminent visitor. The playwright Oscar Wilde brought his family to Worthing and stayed at The Haven, 5 The Esplanade in East Worthing (now the site of a garage). He apparently enjoyed his visit thoroughly, writing *The Importance of Being Earnest* here. When not writing he bathed

100   When playwright Oscar Wilde visited Worthing in 1894 he stayed at no.5 The Esplanade. The terrace, between Brighton Road and the seafront to the east of Splash Point, had been built in 1885. It was demolished in 1967 and replaced with a garage.

101 The annual Regatta was an important occasion in Worthing and events were centred around the Pier. While he was visiting Worthing in 1894 Oscar Wilde presented the prizes at the Regatta.

and spent much of his time on the promenade. He wrote to his friend Lord Alfred Douglas about two young men who had caught his eye, Alphonse and Stephen. Alphonse was a newspaper boy who became his regular companion. The trio went sailing and bathing together. At the annual regatta Wilde presented the prizes for the best-dressed vessels. He commented on how struck he had been by the grace of everything he had seen. He

said that the town had beautiful surroundings, an excellent water supply and plenty of opportunities for pleasure. His comment about the quality of the water was particularly welcome after the previous year's disastrous events.

No late Victorian seaside resort was complete without a bandstand. Worthing's elegant iron 'birdcage' bandstand was built in 1897 where the Lido now stands. Residents and holiday-makers

102 It is a matter of regret that the elegant birdcage bandstand which was built on the seafront in 1897 no longer survives. The military bands that played there were so popular that seats had soon to be built to accommodate those of the listeners who wanted to sit down. Others simply enjoyed the music while strolling along the Pier or promenade.

103   The bandstand was a victim of its own success and was demolished to make way for a much larger Band Enclosure in 1929. Not only could the new enclosure seat much larger audiences but there was also space for dancing. The introduction of an entry charge was a deterrent to some people who were used to enjoying the promenade concerts free of charge.

alike enjoyed countless brass band concerts as they walked along the promenade or sat in deck-chairs to listen. Many of the concerts were given by the Worthing Borough Band under the leadership of Mr. W. Dudley Iveson. The concerts proved so popular that sheltered seating was soon built between the bandstand and the sea. By the 1920s delicate bandstands were no longer fashionable and in 1925 the bandstand was, sadly, demolished to make way for a much larger Band Enclosure. This had a large open area for seating or dancing in front of a covered stage. Once the domed roof over the stage had been added in 1929 the acoustics were such that the music could some-times be heard well inland. People had to pay an entry charge to the new Band Enclosure and this partly destroyed the old informal atmosphere created by the concerts on the old bandstand.

In 1901 the Council built the first electricity generating station in the Borough in High Street. It powered street lights but initially had only eight private customers. This number grew slowly but steadily. Durrington was connected to the supply in the early 1920s. By 1929 the booklet published by the Council to celebrate Greater Worthing could boast that 'Most of the streets are now lighted by electricity and there are over 7,500 private customers'. Worthing's electricity supply was linked to the National Grid in 1931.

Disaster struck the *Royal Sea House Hotel* on the corner of South Street and Marine Parade in May 1901 when it caught fire and was completely gutted. The shell remained standing for over twenty years, surrounded by advertising hoardings. It was eventually demolished, along with shops on the corner of South Street and Montague

Street, to make way for the Arcade which opened in 1925. This has recently been renamed the Royal Arcade.

Since being built in the 1820s, Beach House, on the Brighton Road, has been one of the largest and most attractive houses in the town centre. It has, however, had a somewhat chequered existence. Owned for some years by the Loder family, it was offered to the Council at the reduced price of £20,000. In 1913 grandiose plans were drawn up for the conversion of the Beach House and estate into an elaborate Winter Garden designed to enable Worthing to compete with the year-round attractions on offer at various other resorts. There was considerable debate over whether the Council should buy the estate or use their money to provide an open space in Tarring. In February 1914 there was a referendum of townspeople in which the Winter Garden scheme was defeated by a resounding majority. The future of the house remained uncertain throughout most of the First World War, until it was sold to American playwright Edward Knoblock in 1917. He restored

104 In 1901 the *Royal Sea House Hotel* on the corner of South Street and the seafront was gutted in a spectacular fire. Crowds gathered to watch. The fire brigade was unable to save the hotel which remained on the corner, a useless wreck until it was replaced by the Arcade.

105 The Art Deco-style Arcade was built where the *Royal Sea House Hotel* formerly stood. While its construction led to the removal of the ugly hotel ruin, it also led to the demolition of buildings on the corner of South Street and Montague Street including Lucy Mason's Fancy Bazaar. This photograph was taken in the 1930s.

106 The northern 10-acre section of the Beach House Estate was bought in 1922 and laid out as a park which opened in 1924. The Council bought Beach House and the rest of the grounds in 1927.

the house but then sold it in 1923 to a Mr. Cohen. He, in turn, sold the northern part of the grounds to the Council for £8,500 and they then spent a further £9,000 turning them into a public park. In 1927 the Council bought the house and the rest of the grounds for £16,000.

For nine years the house was empty while an incredible range of uses was considered. These ranged from council offices to a menagerie complete with scenic railway, elephant, camel and llama, a children's hospital or a swimming pool. In 1936-7 it was used to house children who had come to Worthing as refugees from the Spanish Civil War. In 1939 the house was only saved from demolition by the start of the Second World War and it was taken into use as Civil Defence Headquarters. In 1947 the Council again planned to demolish the house but after a public enquiry it was protected with a preservation order. Another eccentric range of uses was proposed over the next few years before the Ministry of Defence took it over in 1952 as an Air Training Corps Headquarters. They left in 1973 and the next wave of proposals followed. Some, such as use as a nuclear fall-out shelter or a casino, were bizarre. There was also a campaign, sadly defeated, to turn it into a museum. It was eventually converted into luxury flats.

Swandean was originally built as a house but in 1896 the Borough leased it as an Isolation Hospital. In 1903 the Borough bought the house and grounds for £2,200. Although it was

107 Swandean was originally built as a house but has been used as a hospital since 1896. Originally designed as an isolation hospital, it has been used for the care of geriatric patients since 1957.

used as an isolation hospital it had no trained fever nurse until 1905. In 1907 a telephone was installed, before which time, if the Matron needed the help of the medical superintendent, she had to cycle to Worthing along wooded and secluded lanes carrying a stout stick on her handlebars to defend herself. In 1908 special blocks to house patients with diphtheria and scarlet fever were built and in 1920 a new tuberculosis block was added. Since 1957-8 it has been used for geriatric patients.

M.W. Shanley, deck-chair and bathing tent owner, had a good eye for what the public wanted in the way of entertainment and opened the town's first cinema in November 1907 at the Winter Hall, formerly the old Congregational Hall, on the corner of Portland Road and Montague Street. It closed in 1923 and Boots now occupies the site. The second cinema was in a room over the

108 A separate block for the care of patients with tuberculosis was opened in the grounds of Swandean in 1920. The verandas were to enable patients to get plenty of fresh air.

109 One of the most attractive buildings remaining along the seafront, the Dome, was built as The Kursaal in 1909 by Swiss entrepreneur Carl A. Seebold. He renamed it the Dome during the First World War as Kursaal sounded too Germanic. It was converted into a cinema which opened in 1922. In spite of various difficulties it has remained a cinema ever since and has great support among the people of Worthing.

110 The northern end of Chapel Road looking south in the early 20th century. The number of advertisements plastering the building on the right comes as a surprise to people who think that this kind of advertising is a relatively recent phenomenon.

Kursaal roller skating rink on the seafront. This had been built by Carl Seebold in 1910 and was renamed the Dome during the First World War. In 1921 Seebold converted the roller skating rink into a 950-seat cinema. After years being leased to a series of companies the Dome was bought in 1963 by the Council, who leased it to a cinema chain. It is a grade 2★ listed building and after years in the balance its future has hopefully been secured by its transfer to a trust dedicated to its preservation and use. Just before the First World War Worthing had its first purpose-built cinema in the Connaught Buildings in Chapel Road.

It was not until 1897 that a new theatre opened in Bath Place to replace the old Ann Street Theatre. Called the New Theatre Royal, it was on the site now occupied by Woolworth's and was converted from the New Assembly Rooms which had been built in 1883. It closed in 1929 and was demolished in 1935. There were many other types of entertainment available in Worthing. The Literary Institute, next to the Winter Hall, was used for lectures, recitals and concerts, Brass Band Concerts were held on the

Pier, in Steyne Gardens and on the seafront, concert parties performed on the seafront near the Pier and, apart from the roller skating rink in the Kursaal, where both men's and women's hockey teams played, there were also rinks in Gratwicke Road and an outdoor one round the South Pavilion on the pier. In 1915 deck-chairs could be hired at 2d. for three hours. Broadwater was not left out of the plans for recreation and learning. In 1890 a Reading Room was built by subscription near the south-east corner of the green. Sadly by 1898 it was hardly being used. In 1900 it was taken over by the Parish Council.

In 1909 members of the Women's Social and Political Union visited Worthing and a crowd gathered for an open-air meeting on waste ground. The crowd of nearly 200 struggled to hear Agnes Kelly speak while people blew horns, rang bells and threw nails in her face. Young boys threw rotten oranges at the women. Women who wanted to form a branch of the National Union of Women's Suffrage Societies held a meeting in January 1910 at the Literary Institute. They were addressed by Clementina Black, who had spoken at meetings all over the country and said she had never been treated as badly as she was in Worthing even though it was meant to be a respectable town. Men blew bugles and released mice into the hall during the meeting. A huge crowd pounded on the doors. In spite of this behaviour the Worthing Women's Franchise Society was set up. It was the first and largest of the suffrage societies established in Worthing. The members of the Society urged voters to support the candidates at local elections who most favoured women's suffrage. Within two years they had 160 members.

Other societies were soon established, some linked to various churches. Men who were in favour of women's suffrage formed the Men's League for Women's Suffrage. By 1913 the Conservative and Unionist Women's Franchise Association was particularly active. Plenty of local women opposed the idea of women's suffrage. Leading local campaigners for it included teachers such as Kate Coast, Headmistress of Worthing High School. Mrs. Ellen Chapman was a member of the Catholic Women's Franchise Society and the Conservative and Unionist Women's Franchise Association. She was the first woman councillor in Worthing and only the eleventh in the whole of England and Wales. She was later the first woman Mayor in Worthing and the first in the south of England.

A dramatic plane crash took place in the sea just beyond the skeleton of the *Metropole Hotel* in 1914. People watched in horror as one of four planes going between Portsmouth and Felixstowe began to descend rapidly. The plane was flown by Flight Commander Rathbone with Leading Telephonist Stirling as passenger. It developed engine trouble and struck the water with force. The plane was badly damaged in the crash but boats immediately set off from the beach and rescued the two men. Another naval seaplane circled and towed the crashed plane to shallow water before flying off fast. In the afternoon a destroyer, a torpedo boat, and a government tug appeared but could not tow the plane away. In the end it was taken apart and sent back by train under the direction of Mr. Wade of Wade's Garage in Chapel Road.

Ellen Chapman was a remarkable woman who was responsible for, or took a major part in, several important episodes in Worthing's development between the wars, including the campaign,

mentioned in Chapter 1, which led to the purchase of Cissbury for the National Trust. As well as being Worthing's first female councillor, in 1910, she urged other women to take their place in local government. In 1914 she was nominated as the next Mayor but some of the councillors felt that the town was not yet ready for a female Mayor and used the excuse of the outbreak of the First World War to bring Alderman J. Farquharson Whyte out of retirement to be Mayor. The majority of councillors considered a female mayor during a war was out of the question, and some even threatened to resign if she were appointed. She eventually became Mayor in 1920 and was re-elected the following year.

In 1920 the Council announced its intention under a British League of Help scheme to adopt the small town of Richebourg L'Avoué near Neuve Chapelle in the Pas de Calais in France. This was designed to repay a debt of honour to France that was felt by many people in this country. In Worthing, the scheme was led by Ellen Chapman, and she wrote to the Mayor of Richebourg to ask how the people of Worthing could help. Richebourg was chosen by Worthing because nearly a thousand men from the Second Battalion of the Royal Sussex Regiment had been killed there in one day in May 1915. In five cemeteries around the town 2,624 British and allied soldiers are buried. The town itself was virtually destroyed during the war, like so many places being fought over again and again. Not one of the 423 houses which had been in the town before the war was left standing by 1920. There was some resistance in France to the scheme but its leaders in England hoped that lasting links would be formed between the adopters and adoptees. This has not been the case.

Ellen Chapman led the fund raising with an immediate contribution of £50 and was keen to promote and participate in a number of fund-raising schemes such as a fancy dress carnival and whist drives. The money was used to buy agricultural tools, seeds, blankets, clothes and household utensils. A few people in Worthing objected to the adoption, saying that Britain had already done enough for France during the war and that people here were poor enough. In reply, Major Fox, one of the organisers of the adoption scheme, said that it was based on the good old English principle of the poor helping the poorer. The Mayor of Richebourg wrote eloquently of

111 Marian Frost was a remarkable woman. She was also, by all accounts, utterly formidable, keeping her staff in the Library and Museum under strict control and achieving a great deal for Worthing through the sheer force of her personality. Her brother William was Mayor of Worthing and in photographs of the two of them he appears to have much the more gentle appearance.

the misery his fellow citizens were enduring, living in the dugouts left by British soldiers while trying to rebuild their community. In 1921 Mrs. Chapman led a delegation of English mayors involved in the scheme to Paris, acting as translator. She also visited Richebourg and found that the devastation was even worse than she had expected. The Mayor, Monsieur Paul Boulainguez, visited Worthing with his son Charles in August 1921. On his return to France he wrote to Worthing Borough Council, 'How I love to carry my thoughts back to Worthing. How I long once more to see that beautiful town of yours … I often think that I have left paradise to return to hell.'

The famous illustrator and author of children's books, Edward Ardizzone, came across Ellen Chapman when he was a young boy. She was his grandmother's best friend and used to descend on his family with her large Pekinese dog. He described both Ellen Chapman and his

grandmother as being stout, red in the face and talking nineteen to the dozen. Among her many other roles she was a magistrate, and Ardizzone recounted a tale of a poor Anglican clergyman who appeared before her on a minor motoring offence to which he had pleaded guilty. Shocked that someone in his position should transgress at all, she gave him a very stern lecture and sentenced him to a month in jail. To the embarrassment of all concerned she was then told by the Clerk of the Court that she had exceeded her powers and had to restrict herself to fining him ten shillings. Ardizzone's brief descriptions of Ellen Chapman bring her vividly alive as an energetic, powerful and enthusiastic person. Most appealing, in one sense, may be the touch of eccentricity that reputedly led her to use her many Pekinese dogs to hunt like beagles across the Downs!

In 1900 a retired doctor from Eastbourne, Dr. Howard Nicholls, wrote to the Council offering to lend his collection of stuffed birds to the town to be displayed in a museum in return for accommodation and insurance. After some negotiation his birds (all of which he had shot and stuffed personally) were installed in the old Council Offices in Rowlands Road. Nicholls took up his position as Honorary Curator and announced he was determined 'to stop the Museum being filled with unsuitable objects'. In practice this meant almost anything that was not a bird. Each bird was displayed in a well-designed setting in its own glass case. The *Worthing Gazette* in 1904 said that Nicholls was proud to claim, 'There are only fourteen species of British gull and he has shot and secured ten of them.'

The local papers complained about the lack of publicity that was given to the Museum in 1901. It opened twice a week and admission was free but Nicholls barred children under 12 unless they were accompanied by a responsible adult. He excluded dogs, sticks and umbrellas completely. Some of the adults admitted were clearly not responsible at all as there were a number of attempts to steal exhibits. The Stormy Petrel was especially popular among would-be thieves and had several narrow escapes.

Another remarkable woman whose work still stands as a memorial to all she did for Worthing was Marian Frost. Daughter of the chemist who owned the Bridge Pharmacy and sister of William Frost, who became Mayor of Worthing, Marian was a formidable woman. She became Assistant

112 The building which housed the Free Library and Museum was designed by H.A. Crouch. This painting by Crouch was done in 1907, before work began on the building. It shows how there were originally porches over both entrances. The old library porch was taken away after it became unstable, leaving the building looking rather lopsided.

Librarian in 1897 when the Library was housed in Richmond House on the corner of Richmond Road and Chapel Road. The house had not really been converted for use as a library but looked, to all intents and purposes, like a house stacked with books. Before long every room was filled with piles of books with very little space and certainly no comfort for staff or readers. Aware that the philanthropist Andrew Carnegie had funded new libraries in other towns she wrote to him in 1902, asking him to pay for a purpose-built library in Worthing. Carnegie refused, on the grounds that there was one already. A Town Poll had been held in 1892 and supported the idea of a new library. Although she came in for some criticism from people who said that she had exceeded her authority, Marian Frost did not let Carnegie off the hook and wrote to him again, meticulously detailing the reasons why she thought he should change his mind. He must have been impressed by her determination and

powers of persuasion as he agreed to pay £5,000, to which he later added another £1,200, for a new library, on condition that the Borough Council would provide the site free of charge and that the Council levied the full rate allowed under the Free Public Libraries Act which would bring in £500 a year. The contract for the project stipulated that 90 per cent of men employed on the building had to come from the unemployed as the Council got a grant from the Unemployment Grants Commission for this. While the new library was being built where Richmond House had formerly stood, the staff and books were moved to a temporary home in Bedford House.

While negotiations with Carnegie were going on, a solicitor approached the Council with an offer from one of his firm's clients who wanted to remain anonymous. This client was offering to pay for a new museum to be built, at the same time as, and adjoining, the

113 Andrew Carnegie visited Worthing in 1909 to be made Honorary Freeman of the Borough in recognition of his generosity in paying for the Free Library to be built in Chapel Road in 1908.

new library. Before long it was a fairly open secret that this anonymous benefactor was none other than Alderman Alfred Cortis. The new building was designed by Henry Crouch and building work started in 1907. The Free Library and Museum was opened in December 1908 by the local MP Sir Henry Aubrey-Fletcher. It poured with rain but, according to the *Worthing Mercury*, 'even the large number of Lady Visitors present were patriotic enough to refrain from comment'. Neither Carnegie nor Cortis was well enough to attend the opening but Carnegie sent a warm message of support. Cortis stipulated that the Museum could not open on Sundays unless a 'poll of Burgesses' was held with a large majority being in favour even though they had been told that Sunday opening was against his wishes.

On Whit Monday, 31 May 1909 Carnegie came to Worthing to be made Freeman of the Borough. The papers reported that he made a charming speech in which he described Worthing as an 'enchanted land'. Cortis, as senior Alderman, presented Carnegie with a gilt casket decorated with enamelled views of the Town Hall and Museum and they all went to lunch at *Warne's Hotel*. A certain number of seats at the lunch were made available to members of the public—at a price.

Marian Frost became the Head Librarian in due course and, in 1919, when the Honorary Curator, Howard Nicholls, retired, she was asked to add the duties of curator to those of librarian. For this she was paid an extra £25 a year. The appointment was not without controversy since one councillor objected strongly to paying a woman to do the work when he knew of an elderly gentleman who would do the job without charge. Luckily the majority of the councillors were more enlightened, as Marian Frost did an excellent job in both the Library and Museum until her retirement.

Alderman Cortis, sadly, died of a heart attack while on his feet, speaking, at a council meeting in 1912. In his will he left his shooting trophies, paintings and a bequest of money to the Museum. After his death his identity as the donor of the Museum was made public.

114 This view of Broadwater Road from the railway bridge was taken only a hundred years ago. Houses had begun to be built on the western side of the road but most of it was still bordered by the open land that separated Broadwater from Worthing.

In 1893 by-laws were passed which set down tough regulations for ensuring that bathing was segregated. By the start of the 20th century the rules were more honoured in the breach than in the observance. Families naturally wanted to be able to enjoy their time on the beach together and not apart. In 1914, in response to public pressure and changes in habit elsewhere, Worthing Council decided to risk a limited experiment allowing mixed bathing from the beach on one evening a week away from the main hotels. Even this was bound with restrictions. Ladies were allowed to bathe alone but men were only permitted if accompanied by one or more ladies. Worthing was one of the last resorts to make this change. Bathing machines were used in Worthing until 1924, when the owner of the last 68 was furious at having his licence withdrawn by the Council. Bathing tents continued to be used for changing in. Beach huts were also introduced and are now under Council ownership with tenure of huts being passed down through generations of the same family.

In 1902 Worthing was expanded to include Tarring and part of Broadwater, bringing the town's population up to 22,617. The population reached 34,000 in 1921 and Worthing started to call itself 'The Seaside town of Grape and Fig'. A first-class 12-month season ticket on the train to London cost £52 3s. 10d. and the Worthing publicity brochure claimed that 'commuting is a pleasure and not a toil'. Few people would say the same today. The brochure also claimed that

115 The churchyard wall is on the right of this picture of Broadwater Street East at the start of the 20th century. At that time it was simply known as Broadwater Street. All the buildings in this picture are still there and relatively unaltered, which is unusual.

116 Mrs. Hilda Booth, the first woman taxi driver in the country, also rode a motorbike and acted as a military driver during the First World War, chauffeuring servicemen from one base to another. In spite of all her experience some Worthing councillors were reluctant to grant her a licence as a taxi driver.

because of Worthing's exceptionally mild climate 'an unusually large number of Anglo-Indians and colonials have selected the town as their permanent home in preference to other resorts'.

117 Hilda Booth also ran a riding stable and provided the ponies which gave countless children their first ride. She kept detailed records relating to all her ponies and took teams of her pupils to compete in events around the south of England.

Mrs. Hilda Booth was the first woman to drive a car in Worthing and the first female taxi driver in Britain. The Council had been split about granting her initial application for a licence, since some of the members thought this was not an appropriate occupation for a woman. Others argued that since she had been an Army driver during the First World War she was experienced enough to drive a taxi in Worthing. She with-drew her two cabs from service in 1936 in protest at the Council's decision to lower fares in response to pleas from other drivers. She also rode a motorbike and ran a riding stable, providing the ponies and carts on which many people, includ-ing the author, had their first ride. For many people a pony or donkey ride was an essential part of a trip to the seaside. It is interesting to note that the Council continued to issue Mrs. Booth with her pony licence throughout the Second World War, even when the seafront was closed.

Worthing's own special form of transport, the Tramocars, made their first appearance in 1924, running between the Pier and Grand Avenue. Tramocars were the brainchild of W.R. (Bill) Gates. He noticed that elderly people found it difficult to climb onto the high platform which buses had so he introduced the single-deck Tramocars. They had solid rubber 20in. tyres, tiller steering and ran on electricity. The flat nature of Worthing town centre was very suitable to this type of vehicle. They were a success and extra routes were added. The fleet of Tramocars was eventually sold to the Southdown Bus Company. The Tramocars were replaced by single-deck buses in 1938.

What in those days was an even more exotic form of transport made an early appearance in Worthing. Shoreham airport was used by a number of early aviators, some of whom made unplanned landings on Worthing beach, much to the delight of onlookers. The level sands led some flyers to land on the beach by design and there were proposals for an air taxi service between Worthing and other towns. Unfortunately it came to nothing.

From at least the early years of the 20th century Italian families have come and settled in Worthing. Many of the traditional family and religious bonds have remained strong, giving the Italian community a sense of identity, although

118 Tramocars may look like characters from a children's story book but they were very popular when then provided a service around Worthing from 1924-38. They were well suited to the level nature of Worthing town centre and their low platform made it easy for elderly passengers to climb on board. The first two Tramocars were eventually joined by 13 others before being replaced by Southdown buses.

the younger generations in particular have integrated fully into the greater population of Worthing. This community is still centred around South Farm Road where there are numerous Italian-owned businesses, including the Piccola

119 A number of planes landed on Worthing beach in the early years of aviation and there were even proposals to set up an air taxi service which came to nothing. This seaplane took passengers on short trips from the beach. Here it can be seen outside *Warne's Hotel*.

120 Popular concerts were held at this bandstand in Steyne Gardens for many years. The heavy prams in this picture from the 1920s are in sharp contrast to the lightweight buggies most parents use today. In the early 20th century Steyne Gardens had many more trees than it does today.

Italia grocery store. Many of the first Italian immigrants came to this country in the hope of finding work. They naturally tended to go to areas where they had contacts who could help them to settle in. How the first Italians came to Worthing, or who they were, however, remains

unclear. Early arrivals set up a co-operative through which they helped each other out, giving support and finding jobs. Initially a large proportion of them found work in the nurseries and glasshouses. Their links with agriculture have persisted and there are distinct, co-operative and hard-working groups of Italians who have adjacent allotments in Worthing where they grow their own vegetables. As in other areas they were quick to exploit a growing British taste for Italian food and a number of families opened very successful restaurants. Once they had settled they were joined by their families, the largest number arriving in the 1950s.

York Terrace, on the seafront east of the Steyne, was one of the early rows of houses to be built in Worthing. In 1899 Number 1, York Terrace was bought by G.H. Warne who converted it into a hotel. By 1908 he had acquired the whole terrace and turned it into a grand hotel complete with ballroom. Warne was a motoring pioneer and early member of the Automobile Club of Great Britain and Ireland, the predecessor of the RAC. It was the first hotel to have its own garage and for years Warne promoted it as the 'Mecca for Motorists'. He also organised car rallies

121 *Warne's Hotel* was the first to have its own garage. Its owner, G.H. Warne, was an enthusiastic early motorist who publicised the hotel as 'The Mecca for Motorists'. Its loss, after two fires and years of uncertainty, is regretted by many people who had hoped that at least the façade would be saved. Winston Churchill, Field Marshal Lord Montgomery, King Edward VII and King George V are among the famous people who stayed at Warne's.

122 At Easter 1913 the main decking of the Pier blew away during a powerful storm. The damage isolated the Southern Pavilion which was quickly nicknamed 'Easter Island'. Boatmen were quick to recognise a good opening and ran boat trips around the wreck. The Pashley brothers also flew over from Shoreham and photographed the Pier.

and the annual motor carnival. Warne became a Borough Councillor and the hotel was used as the venue for numerous civic luncheons and banquets. It finally closed in 1985 and there was discussion about turning it into flats. Before a decision could be reached it was devastated by two appalling fires. For a while it was hoped that any rebuilding would include the original façade but the ruins have now been demolished.

Work was due to start on a new pavilion at the shore end of the Pier in 1913. On Easter Monday the McWhirter Quintet was playing in the South Pavilion. A strong gale was blowing and there were only 30 people in the audience. By 9p.m. they had all left. The winds reached 80m.p.h. and in the end the musicians gave up and joined the audience on the shore just before the deck between the pavilion and the shore collapsed under the force of the wind and waves. The marooned Southern Pavilion was quickly nicknamed 'Easter Island' by the newspapers, which also featured aerial views of it taken by the Pashley brothers flying from Shoreham airport. There was no hesitation in deciding to rebuild the Pier and at the same time the foundations were strengthened and the decking widened. The rebuilding cost £10,000. It was reopened by Lord Mayor of London, Sir T. Vansittart Bowater, Bart., with great pomp on 29 May 1914. The Lord Mayor travelled to

123 It is interesting just how quickly events were commemorated with postcards in the early 20th century. A large number of different views of the wrecked Pier were sold as postcards. The messages on the back of old 'disaster' postcards rarely refer to what is shown in the picture.

Worthing by train but had sent his carriage on ahead so that it could meet him at the station and carry him, his wife and daughter in the procession to the Pier. A public holiday was called and large crowds gathered to watch the opening ceremony. The Pier was decorated with streamers and lights and over 150 guests attended a formal luncheon at *Warne's Hotel* where they were entertained by the Royal Naval Ladies Orchestra.

In 1920, after years of debate, Worthing Corporation finally took the plunge and bought the Pier for £18,978. Five years later they demolished the old kiosks and built a new Pavilion at the landward end. Some people objected to the building of the Pavilion on the grounds that

124 Paper serviettes decorated to commemorate important events and royal anniversaries were popular in the late 19th and early 20th centuries. This one celebrates the re-opening of the Pier in 1914.

125 The Northern Pavilion on the Pier was built in 1926 to echo the design of the Southern Pavilion. In later years it had an ugly canopy added to the front which has recently been removed to reveal the original design of the Pavilion.

it blocked the view of the sea from South Street. It was built on the theme of a garden house and furnished in blue and gold. It was formally opened on 25 June 1926 by the Mayor of Worthing, Walter Gardiner.

In 1916 there were 34¼ miles of glasshouses in Worthing, with four million square feet of glass. The main crops were cucumbers, tomatoes and grapes. These were classed as necessities and not luxuries, with grapes being exported to America in return for hard currency and tomatoes and cucumbers being, in large part, sent to the towns with mines and heavy industries in the north of England and South Wales. Local papers claimed that coal miners relied heavily on Worthing cucumbers for refreshment when they were underground and numerous glasshouse workers gained deferred or total exemption from military service because of the importance of their work. Shortages of food at the time led the Council to encourage allotment holders to keep pigs on their allotments.

With the start of the First World War, all the Germans and Austrians who were living in Worthing in 1914 were declared enemy aliens and had to register under the Aliens Act. There was a fine of £100 for anyone who failed to do so. By the end of August about sixty had registered. In October all 'alien' men between the ages of 17 and 45 were rounded up, marched under armed guard to the station and interned in camps at Aldershot and on Newbury Racecourse.

The Tribunals which assessed men appealing for exemption from military service were held in the Art Gallery from March 1916. The *Worthing Observer* reported that,

> It was an excellent idea of the Mayor's to arrange for the first meeting of the West Sussex Appeal Tribunal to be held in the Art Gallery at the Public Museum—a comfortable and spacious apartment with excellent acoustic properties which enabled the speakers to be quite distinctly heard without unnecessarily raising their voices. This is a great advantage in the transaction of public business. The numerous fine paintings on the walls increased the pleasantness of the surroundings.

In May the *Worthing Mercury* reported that the Town Council wanted to meet there too but the Art Gallery Committee refused as 'the tribunals were a temporary expedient and to hold Council meetings there would be against the donor's

126 Huge crowds thronged the town to celebrate together on Peace Day, 19 July 1919.

intentions'. During the war, women stepped in to fill many of the jobs left vacant by men who had joined the forces. Some people found this hard to accept and Gas Company manager Sidney Stephenson was horrified that some people should slam their doors in the faces of the women he sent out to repair gas fittings, demanding that a man be sent round. Councillor Ellen Chapman's response to this was typically forthright. She said, 'Then I should leave them alone and let them go without light.'

At the end of the war the population of Worthing was 30,000 but many families had lost one or more of their men folk during the hostilities. The anniversary of the Armistice was celebrated throughout the town in 1919. The *Worthing Herald* and the Borough Council collaborated in trying to collect the names of all Worthing residents who had died on active service during the war. Their names were inscribed on a memorial which was unveiled on 11 April 1921 in front of a crowd of around seven thousand. It stood on the corner of Chapel Road and Stoke

127 The War Memorial was unveiled by Field Marshal Sir William Robertson on 11 April 1921 in front of a crowd of 7,000. It originally had a backdrop of gardens but these were removed when the New Town Hall was built in 1933. The Memorial also had to be shifted slightly to make way for the new building and it now stands on a rather bleak corner.

128 At the end of the First World War Worthing was presented with a tank that the Army no longer wanted. This was in recognition of the amount of money Worthing residents had contributed to the war effort. The presentation ceremony took place outside the Old Town Hall and the tank was then taken to a site near the station. A number of other towns were also given tanks. They were all melted down during the Second World War.

Abbot Road in front of the gardens of Tudor Lodge. The memorial had to be moved slightly when the New Town Hall was built in 1933. It is now used to record the names of those local people who have died on active service in all wars from the First World War onwards.

In recognition of the amount of money that had been raised in Worthing during the War the town was presented with a tank at a well-attended ceremony outside the Old Town Hall on 28 October 1919. The tank was then moved to near the station where it stood until the Second World War when it was taken away to be melted down so that the metal could be re-used for making new weapons.

Both before the First World War and in the period between the wars many regiments held annual manoeuvres on the Downs. Some groups camped up on the hills but others came as far in as Tarring. They often paraded through the town during their stay in the area. Metal detectorists still find countless spent bullets and shell cases on the Downs from these exercises.

In 1915 when imports of German and French toys had been halted by the hostilities, a number of small British toy factories were established. One of these was the Worthing Toy Factory which produced large numbers of toys, although not a single one is known to exist today.

129 Before, during and after the First World War the Downs were regularly used for military exercises. Some of those who came here were in territorial regiments. Postcards were often quickly produced and put on sale, presumably so that the soldiers could send them to their families. This relaxed crowd visited Worthing in 1919.

The firm was set up under the Friendly Societies Act and was led by Miss Flora Duke, who designed the toys as well as acting as Company Secretary. Other members of the Board included Mrs. Ellen Chapman as President and Alderman Farquharson Whyte as Treasurer. It was run as a limited liability company with capital of £1,700. It was first set up in the offices of the Franchise Society at 1 Warwick Street, then in a room in the Church Army Home in High Street, then in Beach House, and eventually ended up in Saltley Lodge in Broadwater Road. The women who made the toys worked a 44-hour week and were nicknamed 'Worthing's Dolly Stuffers'. The factory closed on Saturdays.

By 1920 the firm employed 25 women in the factory as well as a number of home workers. The toys were sold to Australia, Africa, America and India and the factory's biggest order was for one hundred gross of a small toy. Their cheapest cost 6d. and the most expensive, £3. They made

Teddy Bears, Dolly Dear dolls in plush, toy monkey, toys coming out of eggs, elephants, tigers, camels, giraffes, rabbits, woolly lambs, hens and pincushions. By 1920 the firm was making two hundred different designs and introduced new ones twice a year. Most of them were fitted with squeakers. The Cat that Walks, Dog Fido, Humpty Dumpty, Mary's Little Lamb and Jibouna, the Elephant in Rompers, were among their successful designs. In 1924 the factory was taken over by Ramsden Brothers of Station Road Works, Worthing, who, among other things, supplied various London wholesalers with goods. A display in the window of Bentall's shop in South Street in *c.*1920 was labelled 'Worthing's rapid climb to fame in Toy Making. Cute Novelties always, Cute local labour always, Cute Prices always. 1920 Bearly six years and at the top'.

A continuing problem in the early years of the 20th century was periodic floods. High tides and heavy rain both caused problems. High tides

130 This award-winning display of toys made at the Worthing Toy Factory was set up in Bentall's window in South Street in 1920. It shows just how many types of soft toy the 'Worthing Dolly Stuffers' made.

flooded over the seafront on a number of occasions, spreading up nearby roads and leading people to take to their boats until the waters subsided. Heavy rains caused people to do the same in Tarring Road in 1915 when a downpour caused the Teville stream to flood. Floods caused by both sea and rain do still happen in Worthing but much less often than they used to.

In the late 1920s many communities in South Wales were left devastated by the closure of the pitheads and steelworks. In September 1928 representatives from the Society of Friends held a meeting to try to find ways of helping some of the distressed areas. This stimulated interest among various groups and on 28 November Mayor William Frost called the first town meeting for many years to consider what to do. The meeting heard that 14,000 children in South Wales needed boots and clothing and that 300 suffered from malnutrition. Worthing decided to concentrate on helping one town and hope that other English towns would follow. On 1 December it officially adopted Brynmawr. Brynmawr is a small town in South Wales, where the Brecon Hills merge with the Black Mountains. In 1928 it had a population of 8,500 and 86 per cent of the workers were unemployed. Fund raising and the transport of aid were led by the Rotary Club and the Society

131 Especially high tides regularly flooded the road along the seafront in the early 20th century. Holding back the water had been a problem for local engineers since the middle of the previous century.

132 Heavy rain could cause dramatic floods inland. This amazing photograph shows the junction of Tarring Road and Heene Road in 1915 after rain caused the culverted Teville stream to flood dramatically.

of Friends. The Mayor of Worthing visited Brynmawr to see for himself what aid was needed. Some of the women in Brynmawr were offered domestic work in Worthing and recuperative holidays in the area were arranged for Welsh children. As usual, when disasters happen, some of those wanting to help concentrated on raising money for toys and Christmas parties for children but the Society of Friends' representative in Brynmawr wrote and asked Worthing to save some money to help with constructive work and

town development which would have a more lasting beneficial effect. The Council in Brynmawr wrote to Worthing to say 'In years to come when things may have altered, we will never forget. We will always treasure the name of Worthing and the generosity you have shown during these desperate times.' Worthing Museum has an inscribed miner's lamp which was presented to the town by the people of Brynmawr as a token of their gratitude.

Six

Greater Worthing, 1929-2000

In 1929 Worthing's boundaries were again extended with the formation of 'Greater Worthing'. Greater Worthing came into being on 21 May and took in land up to Cissbury and included Durrington and Goring. It doubled the population of the Borough. The Worthing coastline was extended to four and a half miles. The occasion was marked by a procession through the town followed by a banquet for dignitaries, including the mayors of neighbouring towns, at *Warne's Hotel*. In the early 20th century no important civic occasion could pass without a banquet at *Warne's*. After lunch the procession reformed and went to each part of the new Borough boundary where the Worthing Military Band played 'selections of music'. The Lord Mayor of London unveiled a new boundary stone at the new northern boundary. The following day groups of schoolchildren were led around to 'beat the bounds' of the Borough. Each group carried their school flag which was then attached to the boundary posts. They sang one verse of the National Anthem and then took the following pledge of loyalty to Worthing:

> I pledge my loyalty to Worthing. I promise to maintain its honour, to obey its just decrees, to contribute cheerfully to its prosperity, to assist its undertakings with

133 One of the events staged to celebrate the creation of Greater Worthing in 1929 was the Beating of the Bounds. Groups of children were sent out to points around the Borough boundary where they raised their school's flag, sang a patriotic song and performed the 'Worthing Yell'.

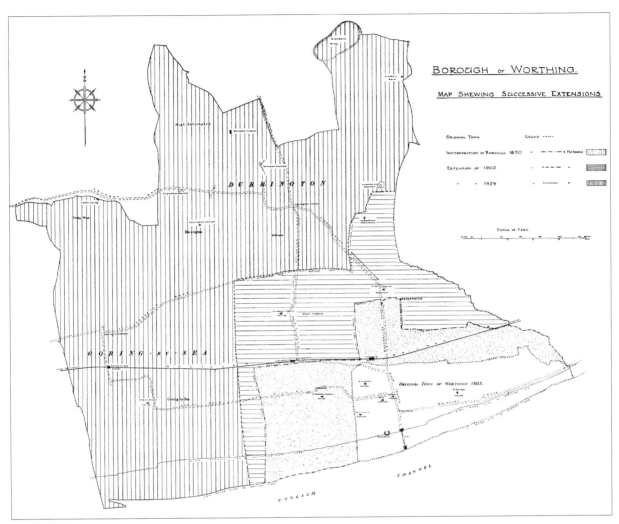

134 Map taken from the brochure issued to mark the expansion of the Borough in 1929 and showing how Worthing had grown over the years before it became Greater Worthing.

diligence, to serve my neighbours with integrity, and to endeavour in every way to be a worthy citizen.

Each child was given a certificate with the oath of loyalty on it. Having reached their allotted point on the boundary they sang a patriotic song, were read a message from the Mayor and despatched a cyclist with a resolution in reply. One pupil was then 'bumped' and the group performed 'The Worthing Yell' (whatever that might be) before returning to the Town Hall for tea. For adults there was dancing in Homefield Park with fireworks.

As in many seaside areas, a shortage of houses in the 1920s-30s was one of the reasons behind the development of a community of mainly theatrical and artistic people living in converted railway carriages, buses, huts and caravans on and just behind the beach. In Worthing this community came to be known as the Goring Colony. It occupied the top of the beach in the area where Marine Crescent and Eirene Road are now and was a cause of anger and frustration among Goring parish councillors before Goring became part of Greater Worthing in 1929. When building spread along that part of the seafront the colony was cleared away. Some of the

135 Part of the Greater Worthing celebrations outside the Pier Pavilion on 21 May 1929.

136 A section of the group of railway carriages, huts and caravans which formed the Goring Beach Colony in the 1920s. The Colony was cleared away when housing development spread to the area in the 1930s.

137 The remains of two London County Council Trailer Trams which had been built into a bungalow in Eirene Avenue, Goring. They were rediscovered when the bungalow was demolished, and taken away to the London Transport Museum.

occupants, however, did not move far, and in the late 1990s workmen demolishing a bungalow in Eirene Road found that it had been built around two London County Council Trailer Trams. The London Transport Museum took them away to add to their collections.

During the inter-war years a clear age imbalance developed in the population of Worthing. At one time 34 per cent of the population was over 65 and this was said to be the highest proportion anywhere in Europe. This is no longer true but it contributed to several of Worthing's popular and affectionate nicknames such as 'the elephants' graveyard', 'God's waiting room' and 'the place people come to die and forget what they came for'. This age imbalance has meant that some of Worthing's priorities for spending have been different from other resorts and led to a belief held by many people that Worthing is a fuddy-duddy town. There were complaints about the lack of facilities for young people: a marked contrast to the mid-19th century when several writers described the town as being ideal for children and the young. Over the years the age imbalance has changed, even though the population is aging nationally, and the town certainly has more to offer young people today than it did in the first decades after the Second World War.

138 The cover from the Council's 1933 brochure shows how the idea of Sunny Worthing was used as the main selling point.

139   The new Town Hall in Chapel Road was opened by Prince George, later the Duke of Kent, in May 1933. It was designed by Charles Cowles Voysey, FRIBA. The Borough's motto carved above the entrance reads, 'Ex terra copium e mare salutem' and means, 'from the land plenty and the sea, health'.

A new town hall was built in 1933 to unite the Council departments which were scattered in various buildings around the town. It was designed by Charles Cowles-Voysey and cost £175,000. With admirable and unrepeated foresight it was made large enough to include spare offices ready for growth. The building also housed the Magistrates' Court where the Gordon Room is now, with rooms for magistrates and barristers and separate rooms for male and female witnesses. A few years later the Assembly Hall, adjoining the Town Hall to the west, was added. Alderman James Gurney Denton, who had been Mayor in 1908 and 1922-4, contributed £40,000 towards the cost of the Assembly Hall. He also gave Denton Gardens. He later left a legacy to the town which was used to add the Denton Lounge (now Café Denton) to the Pier Pavilion in 1959.

Worthing Pier was struck by disaster again on 10 September 1933. An off-duty fireman among the crowds on the beach noticed smoke coming out from under the landing stage at the southern end. He raced to the Fire Station in High Street to raise the alarm but, for some reason, there was a 20-minute delay before the force was called out and by then the fire had got a firm hold and, fanned by a stiff easterly wind, had reached the South Pavilion. The reason for the delay has never been explained. Crowds of holiday-makers rushed to help save what they could of the Pier and, using their bare hands, or whatever tools they could get, ripped up the decking to stop the fire spreading to the pavilion at the landward end of the Pier. Forming a human chain they also passed furniture from the Southern Pavilion onto a car which shuttled to and fro along the Pier, driving the furniture to safety on the promenade. They achieved a huge amount but within half an hour the Southern Pavilion had been gutted by the fire.

140 The Southern Pavilion on the Pier caught fire on Sunday 10 September 1933. Crowds watched in horror as the blaze caught hold. By the time the fire brigade arrived, after a delay that has never been explained, there was little they could do.

141 Seeing the fire, members of the public leapt into action to save as much as they could in the way of furniture, fittings and even the pier decking before being driven back by the intensity of the blaze.

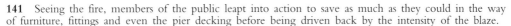

142 The devastation caused by the fire can be clearly seen in this aerial view.

The blaze could be seen from as far away as Beachy Head and the story filled the front page of the next day's *Daily Mirror*. Less than two years later the *Mirror* reported that the Pier had been repaired with a new pavilion which it described as 'the Suntrap of the South Coast'. Facilities in the new building included a solarium complete with ultra-violet lamps. Although it cost £18,000 the Council's insurers only paid out £13,717 after the fire, so the Council had to find the remaining money from its own funds.

The Rivoli Cinema had opened in 1924, and with the opening of the Plaza Cinema in 1933 and the Odeon in 1934 there was now a total of 6,500 cinema seats in Worthing. The Plaza was the largest, with 2,012 seats. It was turned into a Bingo Hall in 1968 and the Odeon was demolished in the 1980s. Simson Fraser and Charles Bell presented their theatrical company at the Connaught in 1932, performing on the stage upstairs in Connaught Buildings. Three years later a new façade

and an Art Deco-style extension were added to the Picturedrome and the cinema was converted into the Connaught Theatre. After years as a successful repertory theatre the Connaught audiences began to decline and the theatre has had a chequered history in recent years. The most recent adaptation is to use it as a cinema most of the time with occasional theatrical performances. The Ritz ballroom in the old Connaught Buildings has been turned into a second cinema that is now much needed in the town. The ever-popular Dome teeters from crisis to crisis, but it is to be hoped that its future as a cinema is now more secure than it has been for some years. The Rivoli caught fire in 1960 and was finally demolished in 1984.

Haile Selassie, Emperor of Ethiopia and Lion of Judah, fled his homeland on 2 May 1936 after the Italian invasion. He sought political asylum in Britain and arrived at *Warne's Hotel* three weeks later. With his entourage he took over the whole front part of the first floor that had been turned

143 'The Suntrap of the South Coast' was how newspapers hailed the Art Deco-style Southern Pavilion which was built on the Pier to replace the one destroyed by fire in 1933. As this picture shows, it had seating areas running around the building on all sides enabling as many people as possible to sunbathe.

144 Many local people have fond memories of trips to the Rivoli Cinema which opened in 1923. It had a restaurant, a sliding roof and a resident orchestra. It suffered a disastrous fire in 1960 after which it was used as an auction room. It was pulled down in the early 1980s when Chapel Road and North Street were widened.

145 These Spanish refugee children were among the many helped by Joan Strange and her colleagues. They stayed in a house at High Salvington.

into one suite and redecorated for the occasion. Detective Inspector Smith of the Special Branch stayed with them. On this occasion they remained for four weeks, returning later for a longer stay. Haile Selassie considered buying three properties in Worthing, Hurst Grange in Parkfield Road, Sunningdale on Marine Parade and a house in Links Road. In the end he bought none of them but stayed in the hotel, leaving finally in June 1940.

In 1937 the Council was considering spending £11,000 on the Museum and Library. Cllr. J.A. Mason was opposed to the idea, saying encouragingly 'there will either be a slump or a war. If there is a war we shan't want any library or museum. If there is a slump we shall get the work done for half the price.'

The British Fascist Party had a regional head-quarters in Worthing and its national leader, Oswald Mosley, came here several times. On each occasion his visit provoked demonstrations by his opponents. The Chief of the Sussex and Hamp-shire League of Fascists from 1930-4 was Captain Charles Bentinck Budd who lived in Grove Road and was Independent councillor for Broadwater in 1934. The Fascists held rallies on the seafront and marched around in fascist uniforms. The confrontations were increasingly violent and after it was alleged that 'shots were fired', the local police raided homes and seized dozens of weapons, mostly air rifles.

When Mosley visited Worthing on 9 October 1934 there was a massive publicity build-up. He arrived in an armoured car surrounded by

146 A row of concrete cubes known as tank traps opposite the rowing club at Splash Point. A few people have sneaked onto the beach, which was supposed to be out of bounds.

blackshirts carrying truncheons and accompanied by a fully staffed ambulance. During the day supporters from all over Sussex had gathered in Worthing to greet him at the Pier Pavilion. Inside he delivered a two-hour diatribe. At 11 o'clock the doors opened and, as the *Worthing Herald* reported, 'there was high-speed guerrilla warfare along the whole way from the seafront to Warwick Street'. The Fascist headquarters were daubed with graffiti. Within a week summonses had been issued against Mosley, Budd and their colleague William Joyce (later known as 'Lord Haw Haw'). They were charged with riotous assembly and committed by Worthing Magistrates for trial at Lewes. There, after two days, Lord Justice Branson dismissed the case, ruling that there was no evidence to go before a jury. During the Second World

War Budd was interned. Mosley visited Worthing again on 16 November 1938 to speak to a capacity audience. In his speech he advocated the resettlement of Jews in uninhabited parts of the world. On this occasion a large police presence kept things quiet.

The arrival of the Second World War was as overwhelming in Worthing as it was anywhere else. From the issue of gasmasks at Beach House in February 1939 (labelled 'the Chamber of Horrors' for the occasion) to the re-opening of the seafront after D-Day, it affected every aspect of life. We are lucky to have three detailed and personal memoirs of that period. Joan Strange, a staunch pacifist, kept a diary throughout the war, which was published in 1989. Worthing Museum has the notebooks kept by Lois Jordan, who was

147   This view of the Pavilion was taken after the beach had been closed and defences had been installed all along the seafront. The pile of rubble and weeds in the foreground appears to conceal the entrance to a shelter or pillbox.

an Air Raid Warden, and Mary Lake, who worked with a Mobile Medical Unit, of their Air Raid Precautions (ARP) activities.

Joan Strange dedicated a lot of her time, energy and what little money she had to helping refugees, first from the Spanish Civil War and then from Europe generally. Five hundred refugees came to Worthing. She worked at housing and caring for them, helping them to adapt to their new environment and to move on to America, Australia or other countries if that was their wish, and setting up 72 Canterbury Road as a house for refugees. She recorded in her diary that some local tradespeople were good to them: Mr. King mended their shoes free of charge, and

Mr. Chippings gave them free haircuts. However, not everyone was so welcoming and in May the outside of the house was daubed 'Jews Get Out', 'Britons before Aliens'. Later, needing to accommodate more refugees, Joan and her associates rented a house in Shakespeare Road as well. After Italy declared war on France and Britain, and detectives rounded up nine Italians living in Worthing who were then interned as enemy aliens, even though some of their families had been in the town for generations, Joan Strange did what she could to keep in contact with them and to help their relatives.

In August 1939 she noticed a large van parked outside the Museum which she rightly presumed was removing its main treasures. Some were taken in specially made lead-lined boxes to a chalk pit at the Gallops in Findon Valley and others, like the most important Council archives, were stored in the Ralli family vault in Broadwater Cemetery. As a pacifist she was very shocked to hear the vicar preach of war as a 'Judicial Act of God'.

On 1 September Worthing was told to prepare to receive 10,000 children who were being evacuated from London. Mr. C.E. Marr, from the Rotary Club, acted as Receiving Officer and made arrangements for the reception and billeting of the children and accompanying adults. He did a very good job in spite of the inevitable difficulties. In the two days before the outbreak of war 10,748 evacuees arrived and on the next another 1,420 came. They were aged 7-12 years old and 12 schools had to be brought into service as clearing centres. Some people were willing to take in evacuees. Others had to be pushed. Each child was given 48 hours' rations and taken to their billet. As the 'Phoney War' unfolded many of them drifted back to their homes in London.

Lois Jordan signed up as an Air Raid Warden in 1940, working at the air-raid shelter in Stoke Abbot Road, which she often referred to as 'the trenches'. She had been one of the first people to enrol as an Air Raid Warden at Beach House in late September 1939 and she served for the rest of the war. When the Senior Warden was elsewhere, or off sick (which was quite often the case), she was in sole charge of the shelter, often at night. The most people she ever had there was over two hundred, although it could have held more. However, in 1943 she put herself forward for Sunday Night Duty, only to be told by the Senior Warden, 'I do not consider that a Lady Warden should be on duty at the Trenches by herself at any time.' He said that she could only do Sunday night duty if her father would accompany her!

During the spring of 1940 many people in Worthing seem to have been doing their best to ignore the war altogether. It is true that the only social events held in the Pier Pavilion were for Air Raid Wardens but visitors still flocked to the town. The Council licensed ponies and donkeys to give rides along the beach, prepared to let out beach huts at 10-15 guineas for the season, and ordered vast amounts of new deck-chair fabric. It also issued its annual publicity brochure for tourists in which it tried hard to encourage even more tourists than

ever to visit the town on the grounds that 'it is in these stressful times that a change of air and scene may be most beneficial'. Their only concession to the war was to admit that the advertised entertainment programme might be subject to 'variation due to the national emergency'.

In May, only a short time after the publication of the brochure, Worthing was in the forefront of the invasion scare. Most of the London children who had been evacuated to 'safety' in Worthing either returned to London or were re-evacuated elsewhere. The Pier was closed and, like other piers around the south and east coasts, had a 40-metre hole blown in its decking to prevent a German landing there. This, incidentally, enabled Mr. Bentall of Worthing to be the first to announce Worthing Pier's dubious claim to fame as the only one which has been 'blown down, burnt down and blown up'. No-one was allowed to sit on the seafront near the Pier. Many of the bathing huts were removed, filled with stones and used to block roads, boats were removed from the beach and bathing was forbidden. Concrete blocks known as 'tank traps', barbed wire and gun emplacements were quickly put in place all along the seafront and in the Lido.

In 1940 Worthing appointed the first female police officer in Sussex; and Gladys Moss eventually served for 21 years. Many people were surprised to see her at first as she rode around on a motorbike, dressed in black leather boots, a blue serge skirt and tunic and a man's flat cap with her badge on it. She lived in a police house in Heene Road. Nurse Mary Lake was part of a Mobile Medical Unit led by Dr. Henry Rosenberg. The group had a van adapted as a mobile hospital which they nicknamed 'Jemima'. 'Jemima' was distinctly temperamental until properly serviced. Mary Lake seemed to tackle every obstacle with great good cheer and her diary of nights on watch is peppered with comments on the lack of food, the board games they all played and the loudness of the Medical Officer's snores. On one occasion one of the sisters, in celebratory mood, apparently danced an Irish jig on her helmet! There was great rejoicing the day they were issued with deck-chairs to sleep in and even more when camp beds finally arrived. The first time they were called to an incident with casualties she said that the injured were overwhelmed by the sheer number of eager volunteers! In spite of the light-hearted tone of Mary Lake's diary, the

148 Aerial photograph taken by a German spy plane during the war, which clearly shows the hole blown in the Pier and the tank traps along the seafront.

unit turned out to help at a number of serious incidents, notably a bombing in Hadley Avenue, and acquitted themselves exceedingly well.

Joan Strange noted that there had been an increase in road accidents due to the blackout and that from 28 June it was an offence not to immobilise a car when leaving it. Leaflets were issued giving instructions on the best way to do this. The government announced fines of £10 or three months in prison for driving without white-painted bumpers and running boards. Two British Restaurants were set up in 1941 staffed by Women's Voluntary Service members (WVS). They were Woolton's Café in the Labour Hall in Lyndhurst Road, and Mason Café at Christchurch Hall, Portland Road, opened by the Mayor Cllr. J.A. Mason. Recognising that appetites were larger than rations, the government expected everyone to eat out, on average, once a month and for many workers to have their main meal at school or at work. British Restaurants were simple but well-furnished canteens providing cheap, nutritious two-course meals with coffee. The initial cost in Worthing was 9d. for a full meal.

ARP officer Captain G. Bailey told the *Worthing Herald* that it was his intention to provide shelters for 10 per cent of Worthing's population. To do more would be too costly. 'After all, Worthing is not likely to be the object of persistent raids and you must be quite reasonable about it.' ... 'And if a high-explosive bomb drops on a home everything will go half a mile in the air and nobody will be any the wiser.' The Council planned to build trench shelters in public gardens without spoiling them. Throughout the war there was criticism from locals and from the Government that Worthing Council failed to provide the expected number of shelters or sirens. The Council was hesitant to spend money on sirens which could be heard on the outskirts of the town, rationalising this decision by claiming that people who lived away from the town centre were not likely to be bombed; events proved them to be wrong. Responding to statements that the deep shelters were being sited for those caught out shopping, Councillor Ward asked why, therefore, one was being planned for Durrington Cemetery? Worthing Museum has a German air photograph taken of the town on which targets and defences are clearly identified. It also gives a good view

of the hole which was blown in the decking of the pier to prevent a German landing.

On 16 August 1940 six German planes were brought down in and around Worthing, including one in Honeysuckle Lane, High Salvington. The first bombs landed on Worthing on 14 September, causing major damage to Mitchell's Bakery, Caffyn's Garage and Wells Bird shop in Chapel Road. There was also minor damage to the Town Hall and some broken windows at the Museum. Between May and October the air-raid warning sirens sounded 120 times. An additional problem was caused by gales that blew mines onto the beach where some of them exploded. In December a bomb landed in the sea near Ham Road and blew a large number of sea bass onto the beach where they were collected and eaten by the soldiers.

On 14 May 1940 Anthony Eden broadcast an appeal to the nation asking for people to enrol in the Local Defence Volunteers. In Worthing the first volunteer reached the Police Station to register only minutes after the broadcast. By 17 May over one thousand men had registered. Like all such units, they were short of weapons, ammunition, training and accommodation. Before long the commander of the local military unit was made aware of their plight and made a building available to them. Once they had cleared out all the rubbish which filled it they were able to get properly organised. While they lacked uniforms, men going on night patrol were advised to wear a light-coloured overcoat and to wear an LDV armband. In due course they became the 5th (Worthing) Battalion of the Sussex Home Guard. Patrols began at once. By the end of June the Battalion had been divided into four Companies, A, B, C and D. Before long an HQ Company was added. Company A was responsible for Signals, B was the Machine-gun Company, C, the Mounted Patrol under Col. Thynne (the men in this patrol providing their own horses), and Company D manned the Naval Observation Post. There was also a Red Cross Nursing Unit.

One very sad report in 1941 noted that the death rate among the war veterans who lived at Gifford House had gone up as men who had fought in the 1914-18 war despaired that all they had suffered had not prevented another war. As the likelihood of an invasion again increased in the spring of 1941 the Government wanted to reduce the number of people living around the

149   A group of Air Raid Wardens with Lois Jordan seventh from the left in the front row.

south and east coasts. During the week of 14 March schools in Worthing closed so that teachers could register children for the Government Evacuation Scheme. In some schools the take-up was as low as 25 per cent. The evacuation took place on 17-19 March. Most of the children from Worthing went to the mining area around Mansfield and Newark in Nottinghamshire and to Thurmaston in Leicestershire. Inevitably they had mixed experiences. For all of them it was a real culture shock. One girl said that it was her 'escape to happiness', another was greeted by a hostess who said, 'Oh dear, a child of 12 and not 15 as I ordered.' Some of the children came back fairly quickly and the last group stayed away until December 1944. A few stayed in the Midlands for good.

Both Cissbury and Highdown were among land requisitioned by the Army during the war and, since the exact locations of their trenches, gun emplacements and dugouts were never properly recorded, they will provide surprises for future generations of archaeologists. Even during the war the Worthing Archaeological Society had an eye to the past as well as the present, and while people were digging for victory they were urged, 'should

you bring any relic to light let the secretary at the museum know about it'.

There was a huge build-up of troops in the area before D-Day in 1944. By April the Downs had almost been taken over by the military and were closed to the public. Not only were Canadian and British troops all around the town but lorries and other equipment lined many of the streets, hidden under trees. With the increase in numbers of people in the town and the growing tension felt by everybody, friction between the Canadian soldiers stationed in Worthing and the residents inevitably led to some nasty incidents, mostly fuelled by too much alcohol. For the most part both groups got on well together and former residents and Canadian soldiers alike have fond memories of getting to know each other.

People watching a film at the Plaza Cinema had a very narrow escape on 17 December 1944. A flight of Lancasters had taken off from Fulbeck in Lincolnshire, heading for Munich on a bombing raid. As they approached Worthing one of the planes developed a fault. The pilot, Flying Officer Edward Essenhigh aged 24, struggled to avoid crashing into the town centre. The Plaza Cinema was in his path as he

150 VE Day was the occasion for numerous street parties in Worthing, as elsewhere. This one was in Howard Street. The pram in the foreground contained Elizabeth Rosenberg whose parents, Henry and Mary Rosenberg, are sitting to the right of the pram. Henry Rosenberg was a popular local doctor who served with a Mobile Medical Unit during the war.

fought to control the plane but he managed to avoid any buildings, crashing onto the beach. The plane exploded on impact. The crew members were all killed and the explosion brought down ceilings in nearby buildings.

After D-Day some restrictions were loosened, much to the relief of the townspeople. The last of the Worthing children who had been evacuated to the Midlands came home, on 17 September the blackout was lifted, and at the end of October work began on filling in some of the trenches on the Downs. In 1945 the Mayor opened the Bowls tournament for the first time since the war had started and said that if the announcement of the end of hostilities

came during the Bowls they would all stop for half an hour as a token of thanksgiving. Victory in Europe (VE Day) was celebrated on 8 May 1945. The Borough Engineer spent £250 on flags and bunting to decorate the town. Twenty-six large flags were stolen at a cost to the Borough of £5. Joan Strange watched planes doing victory rolls over the town. Inevitably there were some people who criticised the way the Council organised the VE Day celebrations. The main complaint seemed to be that no event for children such as a party at the Assembly Hall or Pier Pavilion with ice cream, tea, cakes, music and games had been provided. There were, however, numerous, independent street

151 The removal of the thousands of concrete blocks that had been installed as tank traps during the war was a major undertaking. Hall and Co. did much of this work around Worthing. Although the seafront was cleared, those blocks in outlying farmland were sometimes left as the government grant towards the cost of removing them was inadequate.

parties and a particularly large and popular celebration on Broadwater Green. The *Worthing Herald* announced on 2 May 1945 that the Emergency Feeding Committee had barred daytrippers from British Restaurants, as there was not enough food to feed both them and residents who wanted a meal. Later that month the British Restaurants closed for good.

While Worthing did not suffer bombing on anything like the scale of larger or more industrial towns, the inhabitants nevertheless suffered from the same fear, endless alerts and loss as people elsewhere. Most of the bombs which fell on Worthing were being discarded by pilots who had not dropped them where intended, but the railway

and gasworks were targeted. Among the events which most shocked local people were two occasions on which children in school playgrounds were machine-gunned by German planes. The return to peace, too, was no easier in Worthing than anywhere else. Apart from rebuilding and carrying out repairs the Council had to remove all the defence works in the Borough. In Worthing alone 3,270 concrete 'tank traps' weighing a total of 24,181 tonnes had to be removed. There were also static water tanks, shelters, trenches, pillboxes and other structures, which farmers were paid so little by the government to remove, that many stayed in place or were simply moved a few yards out of the way.

152 'Hyam Already' was the nickname written on the side of the sturdy pillbox in front of the Old Town Hall. In this picture the side towards the camera read 'The Star of Liberation'. On the right of the picture is an air-raid shelter in the middle of the road. It must have occupied a hazardous position during the blackout.

Even before the end of the war there was concern about how people would adapt to peace after the years of wartime stress. An article appeared in the Worthing papers discussing the problems which were likely to face homecoming servicemen and suggesting the government was being too optimistic in saying that there would be no unemployment. The writer highlighted the problem of men who had left junior jobs to join the Services, had got promotion in the forces and thus had raised expectations of what they should return to. It also considered the problem of women who would want to keep the jobs and freedom they had enjoyed during the war. People

were shocked when the papers printed stories about what some of the returning prisoners-of-war had suffered along with a list of all those who were coming home. Another article stressed the priority of getting the seafront re-opened and de-requisitioned, with foreshore properties such as hostelries opened again and the Pier restored (although some spoke of demolishing it). In June travel restrictions were lifted and Worthing was back on the holiday destination list.

A pillbox had been built just in front of the steps of the old Town Hall in South Street. Some wit painted 'Hyam Already' on its side. In January 1945 the decision was taken to remove it but after a whole day with pneumatic drills the workmen had only succeeded in chipping off one corner.

No sooner had the D-Day landings taken place than the Council began lobbying the government for priority status in materials and compensation so that they could replace the deck-chairs which had been lost or damaged during the war. One wonders how these pleas were received by hard-pressed civil servants desperately trying to find materials with which to patch up enough houses for the population. There was no doubt about the significance of deck-chairs to the town, and in 1946 the *Worthing Herald* announced that 'for the first time in seven years Corporation deckchairs made a welcome and comfortable re-appearance and were scattered in hundreds over a mile-long stretch of foreshore'.

After the war was over Jack Parsons, one of the Council's engineers, had to prepare a schedule of the damage caused to the Pier and landing stage by six years of war and neglect so that the Council could make a financial claim against War Damage Commission and reinstate the Pier. This was particularly difficult since access to the southern end was made harder by the gap that had been blown in the middle and by the dangerous state of the structure. They decided to do an inspection from the beach at the low spring tide and then with a boat on rising tides. The Engineer's Assistant (chainman) in 1946 was usually a German prisoner-of-war waiting for repatriation, but this time the job was considered too dangerous under the Geneva Convention, so a recently demobbed Royal Marine Commando, Bill Knight, joined Jack Parsons. Arrangements were made for a fisherman to take them out but on the day he was offered a better paid job and did not turn up. One of the safety boats was therefore made available. As soon as they left the

153 Worthing is probably the only town which has a memorial to carrier pigeons. The memorial, in Beach House Park, was set up by local author Nancy Price and opened in 1949. A few years later Miss Price complained that people were letting their dogs drink from the basin that was meant for birds.

154 This photograph taken from the top of the monstrous Grafton car park gives an unusually clear view into the Lido with the swimming pool glinting in the centre. From the emptiness of the seafront and the angle of the shadows the picture appears to have been taken in the middle of a winter's day. In summer the Lido and seafront would be heaving with people.

beach the boat began to take in water. Knight mentioned it but Jack Parsons said this was normal after the boat had been laid up for a while and had dried out. Water continued to come in faster than they could deal with it. Parsons lifted the stern board and found a jet of water coming in through a plughole. The plug which had been removed to let rainwater drain out while the boat lay on the beach had not been replaced. They rowed for the beach with all haste, Knight sitting in the bow to try to keep the stern out of the water. The water was above the seats by the time they reached the bandstand and they only just made it to the shore. They then went home to dry out. On the following tide they completed the job with a secure plug.

The Council's claim for compensation for war damage to the Pier was accepted but materials were short. They adapted cast-iron water mains as piles and the green-heart timber piles of the landing stage were half of the only shipload of that timber imported into the country in 1947. Worthing may be the only town that has a war memorial specifically for carrier pigeons. The memorial, on a mound in Beach House Park,

consists of two inscribed stones and a stone pool. The inscription on one of the stones says that it was dedicated to 'Warrior birds who gave their lives on active service 1939-45'. It was donated by the writer and actress Nancy Price who lived in High Salvington and was devoted to animals. One of her ways of fund raising for the memorial was to collect and sell all the feathers shed by her parrot 'Boney' for at least half-a-crown each.

As early as 1944 councils up and down the country were putting together seven-year plans for dealing with the aftermath of the war. Worthing was no different. The Council considered a number of proposals, some of which, such as the establishment of more branch libraries, were put into effect. Others would have been very good for the town if they had been put into practice. These included expanding the main library to add new rooms for juniors and adolescents, enlarging some branch libraries, and building several rooms onto the Museum and Art Gallery to include a Water Colour Room and a Black and White Room with adequate storage and work areas. Other recommendations included building new schools and a number of other works

GREATER WORTHING, 1929-2000

155 In the 1870s Mark Anthony Lower wrote that 'The Vale of Findon is magnificent'. Although this photograph was not taken on the sunniest of days it does illustrate what glorious views there were around the Findon Valley before vast numbers of houses were built there in the 1920s and '30s.

that, it was suggested, should take place over a period of seven years. Worthing was allocated a hundred of the prefabricated homes which the government issued after the war.

In 1944 the Worthing Council for Social Services presented a very different report to the Council concentrating on post-war housing needs and the creation of community centres. It recognised that the war had put a stop to the building programmes which the Council had been undertaking, but lamented the lack of low-cost housing in Worthing. Their report claimed that, of the 12,000 houses built in Worthing between the wars, only 768 had been for people on low incomes. It praised the Council's cautious approach to building blocks of flats to house low-income families, while recognising that this policy might need to be reconsidered after the war. They carried out a survey of housing in 18 streets and found that a disturbingly high number of houses lacked electric power points, most people had to

keep their prams in the living room or even bedroom, many had mice, some rats, and 88 per cent had no bathroom at all. It is amazing to think that 5 per cent of those surveyed had no indoor tap and some people had to walk 30 metres to use an outdoor privy. The report stressed the need to take the preferences of the people surveyed and others like them into account before deciding on a post-war housing strategy. They considered the provision of private back gardens and open front gardens, with suitable areas for children to play in, important in any scheme. Remarkably, they also considered the special housing needs of 'bachelors' and elderly people, and the need for the latter to be close to good public transport. At the end of their report they added a plea for increased provision of nursery schools and primary schools in areas occupied by families with young children.

By the late 1950s attendances at the Band Enclosure had fallen dramatically and it was felt

156 Between the wars ribbon development spread out in all directions from the centre of Worthing. This picture, taken in 1939, shows development along Goring Road.

157 The first stages of building a new estate around Rectory Road in Tarring in 1933.

158 By the 1930s many of the older buildings in Broadwater Street West had been replaced or given new shop-fronts. This view is taken looking north and the *Cricketers* pub can be seen half way along the right-hand side of the picture.

there was greater need for a swimming pool. In 1959 it was converted into the Lido at a cost of £13,590. The new pool was opened by two Olympic swimmers, Judy Grinham and Angela Barnwell, followed by a fashion parade of swim-suits and beachwear. Angela Barnwell actually came from Worthing. The ceremony was shown on Southern Television and special arrangements were made to fly the film from Shoreham to Southampton. The pool was 100ft. by 41ft., just over 3ft. 6in. deep at the shallow end and 7ft. 6in. at the deep end. It was unheated and said to be the first pool in Britain lined with blue PVC sheeting. Changing rooms were built at the seaward end of the Lido. Heene Baths, which had become dingy and dated since their war-time use as a store and gas-cleansing station, closed in 1967. The Lido was in turn superseded in 1978 by the building of the Aquarena in Brighton Road. The Lido has now been converted into a family entertainment centre and is still a focal point on the seafront. Entertainment for countless families was also provided at Peter

159 Muir House was built as the rectory for Broadwater church in *c.*1790.

160   Muir House was demolished in 1959 to make way for the ugly parade of shops known as Broadwater
Boulevard which was built in the 1960s.

161   Offington Hall was one of many old buildings to be pulled down in the 1960s.
Throughout the country thousands of grand houses were demolished at this time.
Offington Hall originally had large grounds, all of which have now been built on.

162   Charmandean was built in *c.*1800 and later enlarged. From 1926 it was used as a school until 1954, after which it was allowed to decay. Like many other large buildings it was demolished in the 1960s to make way for housing.

Pan's Playground and at the nearby paddling and boating pools.

Between the wars the town had expanded rapidly with ribbon developments spreading to the north and west through Findon Valley and Goring. Lower cost housing was built on land around South Farm Road which had previously been designated for cemetery use. The Council invested a great deal of effort in selling Worthing as the ideal retirement town on the grounds of its beautiful setting, warm climate and facilities for golf and bowls. This rapid expansion was paralleled by the widespread neglect and decay of many local historic buildings. The 1950s and '60s are notorious here, as in many towns, as the period in which an appalling number of historic buildings were allowed to fall down or were demolished to make way for new developments. Worthing residents still bemoan the destruction of the area around Market Street, the northern side of Ann Street and the Old Town Hall, Offington Hall, Charmandean and the cottage where John Selden was born, as well as many lesser-known buildings, and the construction of Teville Gate, the Guildebourne Centre and the Grafton car park. Recent developments, such as the Montague Centre, while no less controversial than the others in terms of the demolition which took place so that they could be built, are at least more attractive and pleasant to use than their 1970s counterparts. Increased pedestrianisation of the heart of the shopping centre has made it far more pleasant for shoppers and pedestrians but has created controversial disruption to the flow of traffic around roads which were already congested.

163   In the 1960s Worthing Borough Council took full advantage of Worthing's superb levels of sunshine and generally warm climate. This advertising campaign was basic but effective. The Christmas decorations in the background show how dedicated the Council was to attracting visitors throughout the year.

'Sunny Worthing' was the slogan used by the Council in its marketing campaigns for many years. This was based on the fact that in some years Worthing does top the British sunshine league and it is certainly never far from the top. In the early 1960s, when smog was still a serious problem in England, the Council employed men to walk around the smoggy streets of London with sandwich boards bearing slogans such as, 'There's no fog in Sunny Worthing today'.

Local government reorganisation made significant changes to the area in 1974. Many of the responsibilities which had been held by the Borough Council, such as education, libraries and highways, passed to the County Council. Worthing became a District Authority in all but name although it was allowed to retain the honorary title of Borough. One result of the changes was that a new, separate library had to be built. It opened in Richmond Road in 1975 enabling the Museum to expand into some of the space the Library had previously occupied. When the spectre of local government reorganisation loomed again in the 1990s there was the suggestion that Worthing should be amalgamated with Adur and Hove to form what

164 South Street has been redesigned a number of times over the years. This view of the area where the Old Town Hall once stood was taken in the 1980s and the area has since been re-landscaped with the pedestrianisation of South Street.

165 Seaweed being cleared by council workmen from the eastern side of the Pier in 1956. No satisfactory method has ever been found for dealing with the periodic seaweed menace.

166   Some children managed to turn the abundance of seaweed to their advantage. These two used it to make cars on the beach in the 1920s.

167   Peter Pan's Playground at the eastern edge of the seafront was a delightful haven for generations of children with its helter-skelter, swingboats, castle and other attractions.

168   The paddling pool on the seafront in east Worthing, along with the boating pool and the playground, was built on part of the former Beach House Estate in 1937-8. The modern Aquarena now stands beside the pool.

one writer called 'the South Coast Conurbation'. In the end Worthing and West Sussex were unaffected by the reorganisation.

Finally, it is impossible to write a history of Worthing without mentioning the seaweed which has been a periodic problem since at least 1805. A superabundance of seaweed on Worthing beach is a fact of life caused in part by the friable nature of the seabed which provides an ideal home for certain kinds of weed that then get detached by winds and tides and wash ashore in large quantities. Plenty of late Victorian and Edwardian postcards show people enjoying themselves on the beach in spite of the seaweed that surrounds them. Some people have always complained about the smell of the seaweed when it decays and certainly when, in the late 19th century, it was mixed with effluent as well as the fish guts cast aside by the fishermen, it must have been appalling. On the other hand, some 19th-century writers made the seaweed one of the town's main selling points, claiming that the air was particularly

invigorating since it was impregnated with seaweed. Whenever the seaweed arrives a chorus of complaint rises to condemn the Council loudly for failing to solve the problem. This is not fair since they have put a lot of resources into investigating a variety of solutions over the years. The scale of the problem is apparent when you read that if all the weed washed up in 1996 had been carted away it would have filled 60,000 lorries. The same people who find the smell of the seaweed most offensive would certainly have had grounds for complaint if this many lorries had trundled through the town centre carrying loads of decaying seaweed.

Worthing at the start of the 21st century is a town of contrasts. It periodically fills with hoards of bowlers, usually mature and undeniably keen. Worthing is the headquarters of the English Bowling Association and has twice hosted the World Bowls competition. On the other hand, like many southern towns, it plays host to large numbers of young students from all over the world who come here to learn English. It is true that

169   Goring beach as it is today on a warm midsummer's evening.

with the advent of relatively cheap foreign holidays fewer people spend their summer break on the south coast. This is a mixed blessing. Visitors are always welcomed and it is delightful to see the beach full of happy groups in the summer. However, the beach is more pleasant now than it was in the heyday of the British Seaside Holiday when it was almost impossible to find a large enough space on the beach to lie down. It has one of the best shopping centres in the county, thronged with people, but it also has plenty of parks, gardens and other quiet places where it is pleasant to sit, relax and watch the world go by. Above all it has the sea. What attracted people to Worthing in the late 18th century is as wonderful today. At any time of year and in any weather the sea is enthralling to watch. Worthing will continue to be a place to which incomers move, meaning to stay for a few years only to put down deep roots of their own.

Bibliography

Abbreviations

SAC *Sussex Archaeological Collections*, the Journal of the Sussex Archaeological Society

General

Brandon, P., *The South Downs* (Chichester, 1998)
Brandon, P. and Short, B., *The South East from AD1000* (London, 1990)
Brighton Evening Argus
Davies, Roger, *Tarring; A Walk Through its History* (Tarring, 1990)
Elleray, D. Robert, *Worthing: A Pictorial History* (Chichester, 1977)
Elleray, D. Robert, *Worthing: Aspects of Change* (Chichester, 1985)
Elleray, D. Robert, *A Millennium Encyclopaedia of Worthing History* (Worthing, 1999)
Fox Wilson, Frank, *Goring and Highdown* (Goring, 1987)
Gooch, Henry, *The Emergence of Worthing from the Incubator of Time* (Unpublished Manuscript in Worthing Museum, *c.*1947)
Hare, Chris, *Historic Worthing, The Untold Story* (Moreton in the Marsh, 1991)
Kerridge, R.G.P. and Standing, M.R., *Georgian and Victorian Broadwater* (Chichester, 1983)
Leslie, K. and Short, B. (eds.), *An Historical Atlas of Sussex* (Chichester, 1999)
Migeod F.W.H. (ed.), *Worthing, A Survey of Times Past and Present* (Worthing, 1938)
Hudson, T.P. (ed.), *Victoria County History of the County of Sussex Volume VI Part 1* (Chichester, 1983)
Vaughan, J.A.M., *Goring and Ferring Past and Present* (Goring, 1993)
White, Sally, *Worthing in Old Photographs* (Stroud, 1991)
Worthing Gazette
Worthing Herald
Worthing Library's ephemera collection
Worthing Museum and Art Gallery's ephemera collection

Chapter 1   Prehistoric to Roman Worthing

Barber, M., Field, D. and Topping, P., *The Neolithic Flint Mines of England* (Swindon, 1999)
Burstow, P., 'The Prehistory of Highdown Hill', *Sussex County Magazine* (March, 1941)
Burstow, G.P. and Wilson, A.E., 'A Roman Bath at Highdown', *SAC* 80 (1939), pp.63-87
Curwen, E. Cecil, *Prehistoric Sussex* (London, 1930)
Curwen, E. Cecil, *The Archaeology of Sussex* (London, 1954)
Drewett, P., Rudling, D. and Gardiner, M., *The South East to AD1000* (London, 1988)
Lewis, G.D. and Mattingly, H.B., 'A Hoard of Barbarous Radiates from Mill Road', *Numismatic Chronicle*, 7th Series:4, pp.189-99
Pull, John, Unpublished Archive in Worthing Museum and Art Gallery
White, Sally, *Archaeology Around Worthing* (Worthing, 1989)

Chapter 2   Saxon Worthing to 1750

Drewett, P., Rudling, D. and Gardiner, M., *The South East to AD1000* (London, 1988)
Welch, M., *Highdown and its Saxon Cemetery* (Worthing, 1976)
Welch, M., *Early Anglo-Saxon Sussex*, British Archaeological Reports 112 (Oxford, 1983)
White, Sally, *Archaeology Around Worthing* (Worthing, 1989)

Chapter 3   The Royal Seal of Approval, 1750-1850

A Resident, *A Handbook for Worthing and its Vicinity* (Worthing, 1849)
Elleray, D. Robert, *Worthing Theatres 1780-1984* (Worthing, 1985)
Elleray, D. Robert, *St Paul's Church* (Worthing, 1999)
Evans, John, *A Picture of Worthing* (London, first edn. 1805, second edn. 1814)
Hufton, G. and Baird, E., *Scarecrows Legion, Smuggling in Kent and Sussex* (Sittingbourne, 1983)
Norwood, J., *Salvington Mill* (Worthing, 1987)
Philp, Roy, *The Coast Blockade. The Royal Navy's War on Smugglers in Kent and Sussex 1817-31* (Horsham, 1999)
Shearsmith, John, *A Topographical Description of Worthing ... To Which is Prefixed a Concise Essay on Cold and Warm Bathing* (Worthing, 1824)
Smail, H., *Warwick House*, Notable Houses of Worthing 5 (Worthing, 1952)

Chapter 4   'The Most Innocent Spot on the Whole South Coast', 1850-90

Beswick, Molly, *Brickmaking in Sussex. A History and Gazetteer* (Midhurst, 1993)
Black's Guide to the South-Eastern Counties of England. Sussex (Edinburgh, 1861)
Blann, Rob, *A Town's Pride. Victorian Lifeboatmen and their Community* (Worthing, 1990)
Holden, Paul, *Typhoid, Bombs and Matron. The History of Worthing Hospital* (Worthing, 1992)
Lower, M.A., *The Visitor's Complete Guide to Worthing (The Madeira Of England) and its Neighbourhood* (Worthing, third edn., 1874)
Salvation Army Scrapbook. Album of cuttings from various newspapers collected by the Chief Constable in 1883-4. Worthing Museum and Art Gallery Accession number 1976/202
Snewin, Edward, *Glimpses of Worthing, as narrated by Edward Snewin and Prepared for publication by an Old Inhabitant* (Worthing, 1900)
Snewin, Edward, *Glimpses of Worthing, introduced and annotated by Henfrey Smail* (Worthing, 1945)
White, Sally, *Worthing Pier, A History* (Worthing, 1996)
Worthing Pier Co. Ltd, Minute Books in Worthing Museum and Art Gallery

Chapter 5   'Seaside Town of Grape and Fig', 1891-1929

Anon., *A Descriptive Account of Worthing Illustrated* (Worthing, *c.*1895)
Ardizzone, E., *The Young Ardizzone. An Autobiographical Fragment* (London, 1970)
Blann, Rob, *Edwardian Worthing. Eventful Era in a Seaside Town* (Worthing, 1991)
Cave, Frank, *Rotary In Worthing 1922-47* (Worthing, 1947)
Cresy, Edward, *Report ... on a preliminary Enquiry into the sewerage, drainage and supply of water, and the sanitary conditions of the inhabitants of Worthing* (London, 1850)
Frost, M. and Carnegie, A., Copies of correspondence in Worthing Museum and Art Gallery
Holden, Paul, *Brave Lads of Sunny Worthing* (Eastbourne, 1991)
Holden, Paul, *Typhoid, Bombs and Matron. The History of Worthing Hospital* (Worthing, 1992)
Kelly, Charles, *Report on the Enteric Fever in 1893 in the Borough of Worthing, Broadwater and West Tarring* (Brighton, 1894)
Montgomery, I., *The Italians in Worthing* (Unpublished Project, 1999)
Smail, Henfrey, *Beach House*, Notable Houses of Worthing 1 (Worthing, 1947)
Ward and Lock, *Illustrated Guide to, and Popular History of Brighton, Worthing, Lewes, with Excursions in the Neighbourhood* (London, 1891)

Chapter 6   Greater Worthing, 1929-2000

Clarke, C. and Taylor, R., *Worthing at War* (Eastbourne, 1989)
Jordan, Lois, Manuscript Diary at Worthing Museum and Art Gallery, Accession number 1984/427
Lake, M., Manuscript Diary at Worthing Museum and Art Gallery, Accession number 1993/218
Parsons, Jack, Personal letter, 1996
Strange, Joan, *Despatches from the Home Front* (Tunbridge Wells, 1989)
Watts, Jack, *Old Worthing as I remember it 1906-20* (Worthing, 1982)
Worthing Borough Council, Annual guidebooks including 1940
Worthing Borough Council Minutes, 1939-47
Worthing Council for Social Services, *Homes of Tomorrow* (Worthing, 1944)

Index

References in **bold** refer to pages on which there are illustrations.

TO BE LET,

UNFURNISHED,

IN THE

Village of Broadwater,

A NEAT

COTTAGE,

CONTAINING

Three Sitting and Six Bed Rooms, with Chaise House, Stable, small Garden, &c.

For particulars apply to Mr. BLAKER, Builder, Chapel Street, Worthing; or to Mr. I. PRICE, near Broadwater Church.

Moore and Wilkins, Printer   12, Warwick Street, Worthing.